HEAVY METAL
THE STORY IN PICTURES

HEAVY METAL

THE STORY IN PICTURES

RICO CONNING

CHARTWELL
BOOKS

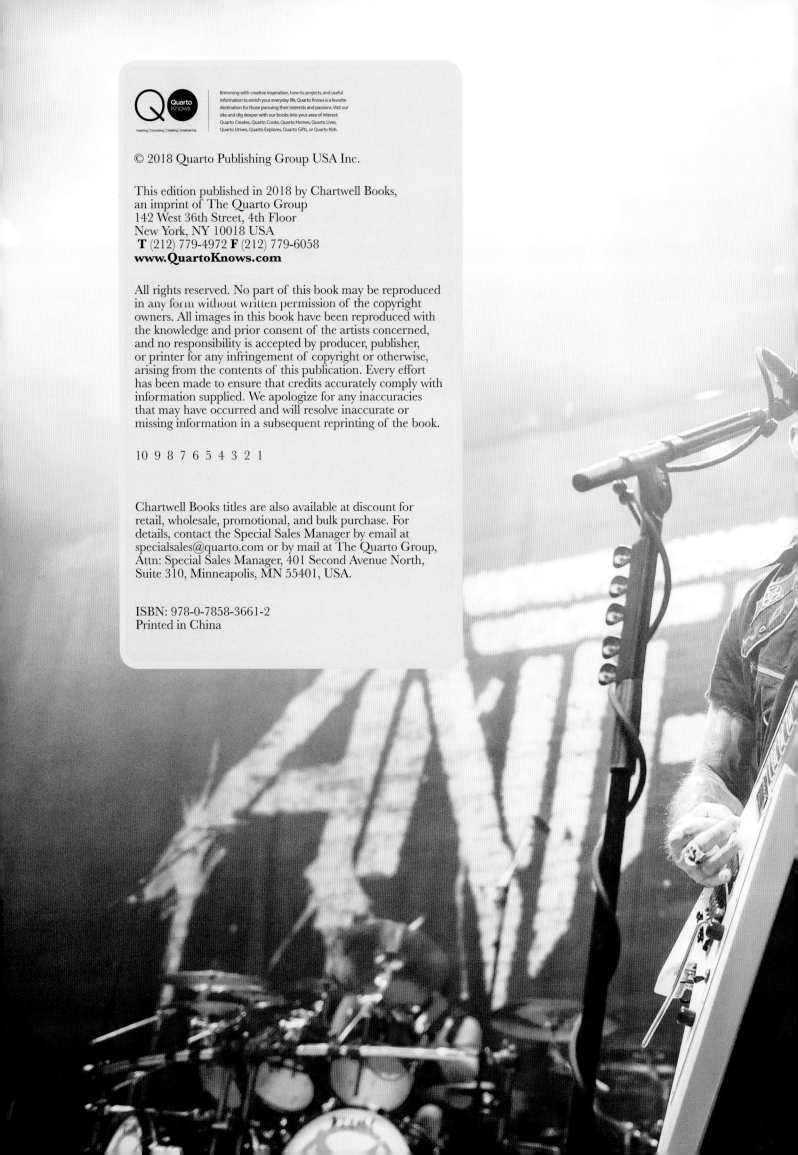

© 2018 Quarto Publishing Group USA Inc.

This edition published in 2018 by Chartwell Books,
an imprint of The Quarto Group
142 West 36th Street, 4th Floor
New York, NY 10018 USA
T (212) 779-4972 **F** (212) 779-6058
www.QuartoKnows.com

10 9 8 7 6 5 4 3 2 1

Chartwell Books titles are also available at discount for retail, wholesale, promotional, and bulk purchase. For details, contact the Special Sales Manager by email at specialsales@quarto.com or by mail at The Quarto Group, Attn: Special Sales Manager, 401 Second Avenue North, Suite 310, Minneapolis, MN 55401, USA.

ISBN: 978-0-7858-3661-2
Printed in China

CONTENTS

INTRODUCTION

The 1950s saw the postwar generation throw off the musical constraints of their parents and embrace rock 'n' roll. This surge in the popularity of electric music coincided with a surge in personal wealth. Soon after, the atmosphere in the 1960s was electrified by a protest movement that culminated in massive marches against the Vietnam War and for CND. Taking all of these influences into account, it's little wonder that there was a revolution in music.

There were three main stages in the development of Heavy Metal. First, the rough and ready approach of **The Beatles** and the use of distorted guitar tones combined with repetitive guitar riffs pioneered by the likes of **The Kinks** and **The Who** in the early 1960s. They were followed by the heavier blues sounds of **Cream** and **The Jimi Hendrix Experience**. Then American bands like **Blue Cheer** simplified and hardened that sound.

The second tine of the fork was Progressive Rock, which found its most extreme acts in **King Crimson** and **Van Der Graaf Generator**, but which really flowered in the early to mid-1970s with more accessible acts like **Yes** and **Genesis**. While these bands sometimes choked on their own virtuosity, they lived on in contributions to other genres.

Finally, there were the Surf Rock and Garage Rock traditions, beginning with half-American Indian **Link Wray** and leading through surf guitar champion **Dick Dale**, both users of distortion. Psychedelic punk bands such as **Count Five** and **The Thirteenth Floor Elevators** and semi-punkers like **Love** and **The Trees** are worth mentioning, but even more of an inspiration were the first dark rock bands, **The Doors** and **The Velvet Underground.** Where other bands had focused on love and peace **The Doors** and in particular singer Jim Morrison brought a Nietzsche-inspired morbid subconscious element to rock music. **The Velvet Underground** brought avant-garde noise to the musical equation.

By 1969, all of these influences had contributed to the explosion of hard rock and proto-metal represented by **Led Zeppelin**, **Deep Purple**, and **Black Sabbath**, at the same time as the development of distorted, power-chord based technical music from **King Crimson**. This year was thus the watershed for loud forms of rock, which would lead to Heavy Metal. In February 1970, **Black Sabbath** released their first album and the die was cast.

In the early 1970s, as Heavy Metal gained in popularity, bands found themselves playing to bigger and bigger audiences. Advances in amplification technology, particularly from British amp builder Marshall, enabled bands like **Grand Funk Railroad** to assail their stadium crowds with blistering volume levels.

For many, the stadium rock of the mid-1970s got a bit too big for its britches. At the same time, while the production advances evident in such albums as *The Dark Side of the Moon* from **Pink Floyd** were not to be dismissed, there was also an inevitable reaction against this sophistry from some of the youngsters coming up at the time. The New Wave and Punk Rock movements of the mid-1970s drew on the artiness of **The Velvet Underground**, but also on the brutal primal quality of **Iggy Pop**, and this stripped-down aesthetic extended to many of the

Page 1: GWAR—along with **Cradle of Filth**, **CKY**, and **Vains of Jenna**—was one of the metal bands to headline the Viva La Bam tour of 2007. Here they are at Roseland Ballroom in New York in November 2007.

Pages 2/3: Devil horns from the crowd at Helifest, Clisson, France.

Pages 4/5: Heavy Metal is a worldwide genre—here Scott Ian of Thrash Metal **Anthrax** is performing in November 2015. They formed in New York back in 1981 and despite a few changes in line-up are still thrilling their fans well into the new millennium and don't look like stopping any time soon.

Right: Heavy Metal is big news in festivals worldwide. Here **Motörhead's** Mikkey Dee on day two of Download Festival 2013 at Donnington Park, one of two major annual British summer rock and metal events (the other is Sonisphere). These feature metal bands such as **Slipknot**, **Judas Priest**, **Five Finger Death Punch**, **Mötley Crüe**, and **Rise Against**.

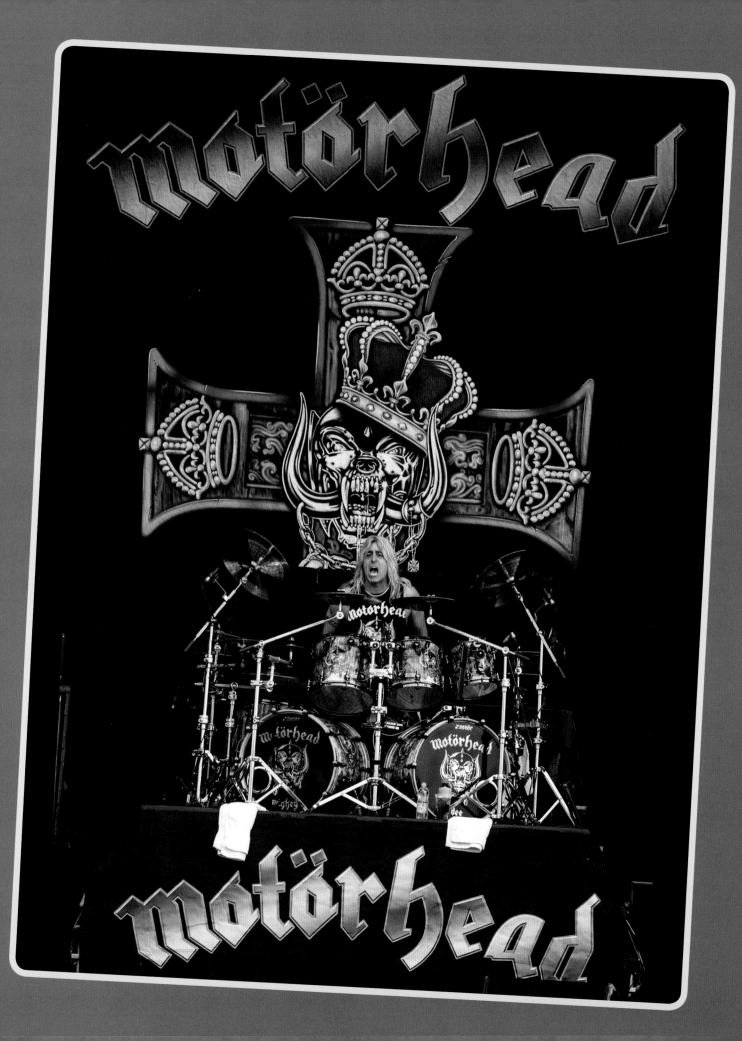

If heavy metal bands ruled the world, we'd be a lot better off

Bruce Dickinson of **Iron Maiden**

newer metal bands of the time. In the late 1970s and early 1980s, a movement coalesced in the UK, "The New Wave of British Heavy Metal" represented by such bands as **Motörhead**, **Saxon**, and **Slayer**.

In the 1980s metal music benefitted disproportionately from the advent of MTV, which was particularly enamored with the Glam Metal bands of the time, with their flashy image and tales of rockin' hedonism. UK metal bands also generally did well from MTV and the likes of **Iron Maiden** and **Def Leppard** became big acts in the US.

The Thrash Metal that sprung up in the US in the early 1980s led by the likes of **Metallica** all but swept everything before it. While some bands clove to the traditional metal elements of the pioneers, Thrash Metal brought an "anything goes as long as it's heavy" attitude which helped to spawn the massively varied scene that we have today.

Later in the 1980s, alternative and industrial music began to have an influence on metal bands. **The Red Hot Chile Peppers** and **Faith No More** had funk and hip hop influences permeating their music. In the 1990s, this trend would produce such vital bands as **Rage Against the Machine** and **System of a Down**. Meanwhile in America's Northwest, the Grunge movement took things back to basics.

Another big influence was classical and medieval music. While the burgeoning Symphonic and Progressive Metal scenes looked to baroque composers such as **Bach** for inspiration, the Black Metal bands in Norway like **Mayhem** and **Satyricon** looked to European music's dark early days to help with their complex musical atmospheres.

By the turn of the century there was a type of metal for everyone, from the darkest Doom Metal to the brightest Christian or Folk Metal, from the pop riffing of Nu Metal to the noise and chaos of Avant-Garde Metal. Genres split into subgenres, which then split even further. We will attempt to deal with the principal ones in this book. If there are exclusions, please excuse us, for Metal is truly a music that contains multitudes.

1. THE 1960s

RAW MATERIALS

Nobody seems quite sure how Willie Kizard's amp got damaged. Bandleader Ike Turner said it got rained on. Willie (guitarist for Ike's band) said it fell off the roof of his car. Whichever it was, the distorted sound that was subsequently used on the big 1951 hit "Rocket 88" was the buzz heard around the world.

However, it wasn't until 1964 that Dave Davies repeated the injured amp trick (this time intentionally with a razorblade) to get the urgent, in-your-face guitar sound of **The Kinks**' big hit "You Really Got Me."

Guitar, amplifier, and effect box maker Gibson USA had already put the sound into a box called the Fuzz Tone, and the first big hit to have it was "Satisfaction" by **The Rolling Stones**. Later that year, **The Who** released "My Generation" with its elements of "auto destruction," another bellwether recording. Meanwhile **The Dave Clark Five** with its "Tottenham Sound" pioneered a pounding, percussive approach with echo-drenched vocals.

Things really kicked off in 1966. **The Beatles** revolutionized the album form with *Revolver*. Jimi Hendrix arrived in London and formed **The Jimi Hendrix Experience**. **Cream** formed with guitar maestro Eric Clapton and released their debut, *Fresh Cream*. Over in New York, **The Velvet Underground** recorded their debut album *The Velvet Underground and Nico*. Ignored at the time, it was a blueprint for later Alternative Rock, and influenced later Alternative Metal genres such as Industrial and Avant-Garde.

In 1967, Jimi Hendrix released his astonishing first two albums: *Are You Experienced?* and *Axis: Bold As Love*. **The Beatles** released their celebrated concept album *Sgt. Pepper's Lonely Hearts Club Band*. **The Doors** released their eponymous debut. **The Velvet Underground** recorded noise rock classic *White Light/White Heat*. **Pink Floyd**'s *Interstellar Overdrive* was another milestone. **Vanilla Fudge** slowed things way down, setting the scene for **Black Sabbath**. **The Who** pushed the boundaries in their own way with hit single "I Can See For Miles."

In 1968, US bands **Steppenwolf**, **Iron Butterfly**, and **Blue Cheer** released records that pushed the heaviness quotient further than before. **Deep Purple** released their debut *Shades Of Deep Purple*. The **New Yardbirds** became **Led Zeppelin** and started gigging. Arthur Brown of Whitby, Yorkshire, revolutionized the use of theatrics and face paint with his band **The Crazy World Of Arthur Brown**.

In 1969, **Led Zeppelin** released their first two albums, arguably the most influential ever to the development of Heavy Metal. **The Beatles**' "I Want You (She's So Heavy)" was an early precursor of Grunge. In the USA, Detroit's **MC5** and Iggy Pop's **The Stooges** released albums that were highly influential for Glam Rock, and later, New Wave and Alternative Rock and Metal. **Black Sabbath** formed, and **King Crimson** released classic debut *In The Court Of The Crimson King*. The stage was set.

They credited us with the birth of that sort of heavy metal thing. Well, if that's the case, there should be an immediate abortion.

Ginger Baker of **Cream**

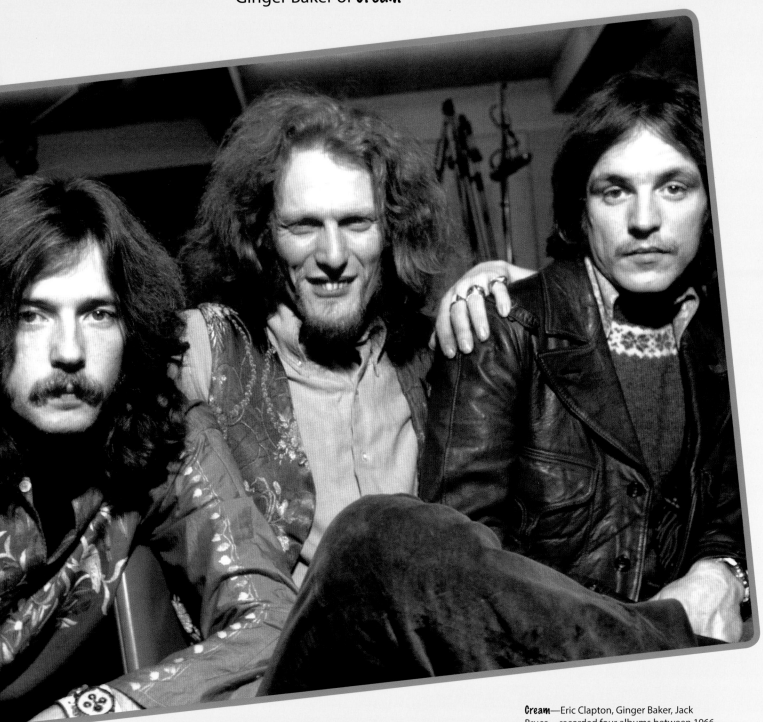

Cream—Eric Clapton, Ginger Baker, Jack Bruce—recorded four albums between 1966 and 1969 and were hugely influential in the early years of Heavy Metal.

TIMELINE

1960

August
The Beatles begin a three-month residency in Hamburg, Germany, and hone their raw but melodic style

1961

September
"Let's Go Trippin'" by Dick Dale and the Del-Tones is the first Surf Rock instrumental

1962

January
Gibson USA release the Fuzz Tone, guitar distortion in a box

April
Portland's The Kingsmen record the raw, riff-driven "Louie Louie"

July
The Rolling Stones play their first gig at the Marquee Club in London

1963

February
The Beatles record debut album *Please Please Me*

October
Eric Clapton joins The Yardbirds

1964

April
The Dave Clarke Five's "Glad All Over" hits #1 in the UK and #6 in the US . "The Tottenham Sound" features a big percussive onslaught and echoed vocals

August
"You Really Got Me" by The Kinks combines a "Louie-Louie" style riff with Dave Davies' distorted guitar sound

November
"I Feel Fine" by The Beatles opens with a burst of guitar feedback

1965

March
Eric Clapton leaves The Yardbirds, is replaced by Jeff Beck

June
Keith Richards uses the Fuzz Tone sound on the riff for "Satisfaction" by The Rolling Stones

October
The Who's "My Generation" features a new level of aggressive onslaught

1966

April
"Wild Thing" by The Troggs is a riff-driven classic

June
Jimmy Page joins The Yardbirds, initially as bassist

The Count Five from California release "Psychotic Reaction," early Psychedelic Punk

July
Eric Clapton forms Cream with Ginger Baker and Jack Bruce

August
The Beatles release the revolutionary *Revolver*

October
Jimi Hendrix arrives in London, forms The Jimi Hendrix Experience

November
Jeff Beck leaves The Yardbirds. Jimmy Page takes over on lead guitar

December
Cream debut album *Fresh Cream* is released

1967

January
Eponymous first album by The Doors released

March
The Velvet Underground and Nico is released, a big influence on subsequent Glam, Punk, and Alternative Rock, and Metal

May
The Jimi Hendrix Experience release debut album *Are You Experienced?*

1967

June
The Beatles' *Sgt. Pepper* is an early example of the "concept album"

August
New York's **Vanilla Fudge** release eponymous debut, featuring slowed-down, heavied-up arrangements that are highly influential

September
"I Can See For Miles" is the biggest US hit for **The Who**

November
Cream's *Disraeli Gears* is produced by Felix Pappalardi, later of **Mountain**

December
Axis: Bold As Love is the second album by **The Jimi Hendrix Experience**

1968

January
Blue Cheer from San Francisco release debut album *Vincebus Eruptus*. Hit "Summertime Blues" is often cited as the first Heavy Metal single

Steppenwolf song "Born To Be Wild" includes first use of the term "heavy metal"

The Velvet Underground release noise rock classic *White Light/White Heat*

June
Iron Butterfly release *In-A-Gadda-Da-Vida*. It will become the world's thirty-first best-selling album

The Crazy World of Arthur Brown predates the rock theatrics of **Alice Cooper** and **Kiss**

July
Deep Purple release debut album *Shades of Deep Purple*

August
Cream's *Wheels Of Fire* becomes the world's first multiplatinum-selling double album

September
Jimmy Page recruits Robert Plant and John Paul Jones, play first gig as **The New Yardbirds**

October
The New Yardbirds become **Led Zeppelin**

Electric Ladyland is the third and final album from **The Jimi Hendrix Experience**

November
The Beatles release eponymous double *White Album*. It includes proto-metal roar "Helter Skelter"

December
Led Zeppelin's US concert debut in Denver

1969

January
Tony Iommi returns to Birmingham band **Earth**, soon to become **Black Sabbath**

February
MC5 debut album is *Kick Out the Jams*, recorded live

Goodbye Cream sees the end of the supergroup **Cream**

March
Led Zeppelin's eponymous debut released

July
Ian Gillan's live debut with **Deep Purple**

October
King Crimson debut album *In The Court of The Crimson King* includes signature song "21st Century Schizoid Man"

Led Zeppelin II released– the blueprint for Heavy Metal albums of the future

November
Hawkwind formed

Deep Purple definitely belongs in the Rock and Roll Hall of Fame. 'Cause they had great songs, great musicianship, they had an impact, and they're a huge influence on the heavy metal community as a whole

Kirk Hammett of **Metallica**

Above: Members of **Blue Cheer**—Dickie Peterson (top, bass), Leigh Stephens (guitar, right), and Paul Whaley (drums, sitting)—pose for a late-1960s portrait. Their cover of "In the Summertime" is often put forward as the first Heavy Metal single.

Opposite, Above Left: "Heavy Metal Thunder"—the first mention of the term came in the brilliant "Easy Rider." **Steppenwolf** (L–R: Goldy McJohn, Rushton Moreve, and John Kay, (Michael Monarch, just out of shot) at Steve Paul's New York nightclub The Scene on June 11, 1968 in New York.

Opposite, Above Right: The late, great, **Jimi Hendrix** at the Woburn Pop Festival, in August 1968.

Opposite, Below: **MC5** recording their debut album *Kick Out The Jams* live in Detroit in October 1968. More punk than Heavy Metal, **MC5** were received pretty unfavorably by the people who today rate them highly.

I like music that's more offensive. I like it to sound like nails on a blackboard, get me wild.

Iggy Pop

Main Photo: Iggy Pop was an early proponent of extreme live shows and is said to have invented stage diving. His own blood was an important part of his act.

Above: Nobody could call **The Beatles** Heavy Metal, but songs like "Helter Skelter" and "Why Don't We Do it in the Road" opened some people's eyes to the potential power. This photo shows their last ever live performance, on January 30, 1969, on the rooftop of the Apple Organization building. They were filming the documentary, *Let It Be* on Savile Row, London, England.

Right: Corky Laing of the hard rock outfit **Mountain** drumming at the Musikhalle, Hamburg, in April 1973. He has been an intermittent member of the band between 1969 until 2010.

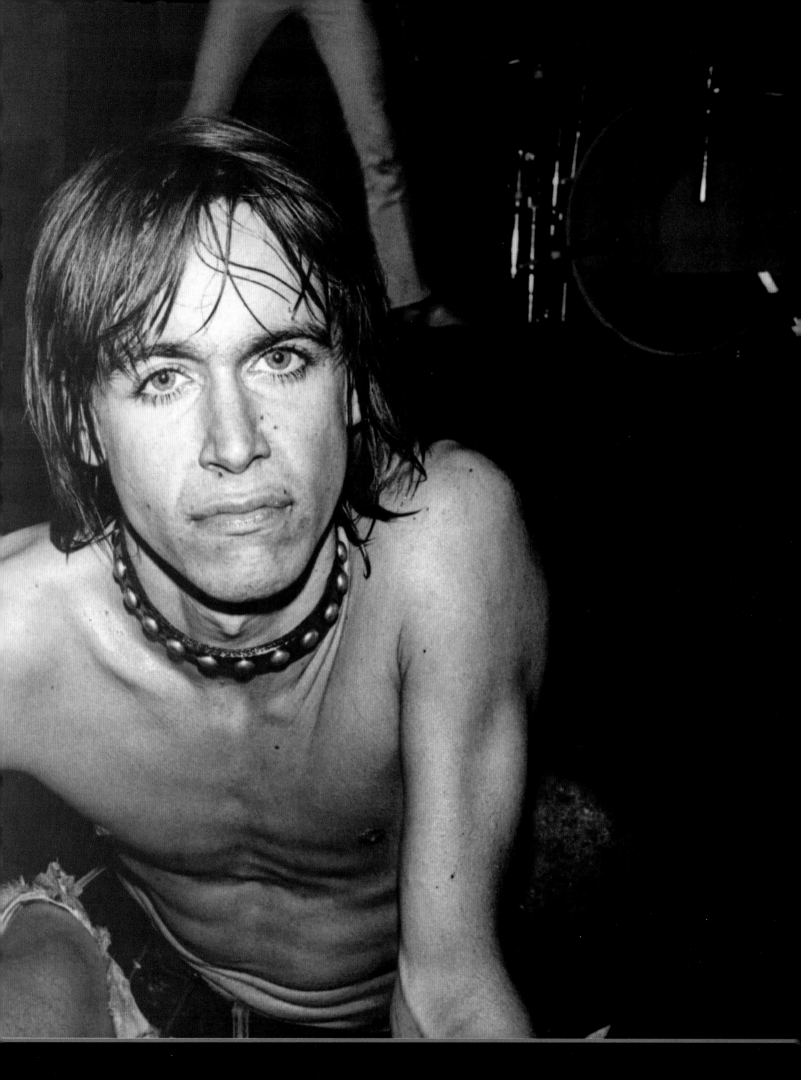

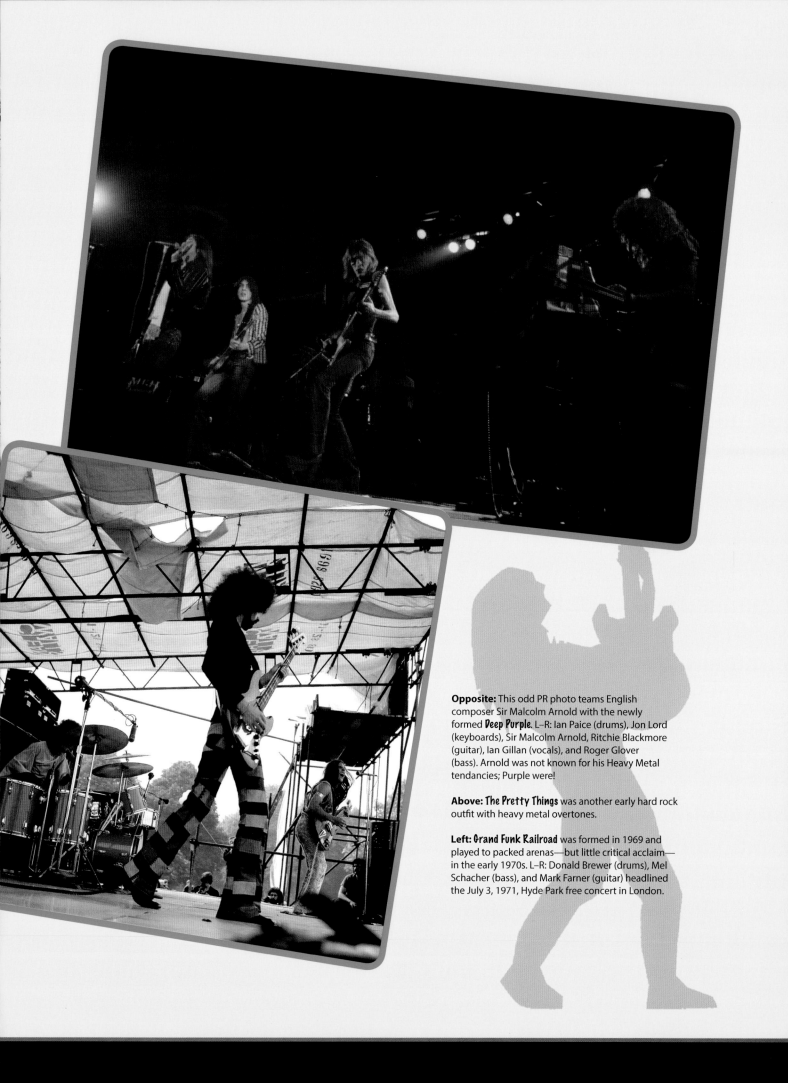

Opposite: This odd PR photo teams English composer Sir Malcolm Arnold with the newly formed **Deep Purple**. L–R: Ian Paice (drums), Jon Lord (keyboards), Sir Malcolm Arnold, Ritchie Blackmore (guitar), Ian Gillan (vocals), and Roger Glover (bass). Arnold was not known for his Heavy Metal tendancies; Purple were!

Above: The Pretty Things was another early hard rock outfit with heavy metal overtones.

Left: Grand Funk Railroad was formed in 1969 and played to packed arenas—but little critical acclaim—in the early 1970s. L–R: Donald Brewer (drums), Mel Schacher (bass), and Mark Farner (guitar) headlined the July 3, 1971, Hyde Park free concert in London.

2. THE 1970s
HARD ROCK GETS HEAVIER

Tony Iommi was 17 when he lost the tips of two fingers in an accident at the steel mill where he worked. He'd been playing the guitar for a couple of years when doctors told him he'd never play again. He was in despair until the factory foreman played him a tape of **Django Reinhart**, who became a guitar maestro after suffering a similar accident. Inspired, Tony found his own way of playing guitar by down-tuning the strings and using bar chords.

Thus the chugging, power chord-based sound of **Black Sabbath** was born. When their first album was released on Friday, February 13, 1970, they didn't exactly birth Heavy Metal, for the foundations were already laid, but they brought a new attitude of inclusivity, a sound that was more attainable than that of the instrumental maestros of **Led Zeppelin** and **Deep Purple**.

In the United States, the Heavy Metal mantle was taken up by arena rock trailblazers **Grand Funk Railroad**. In turn, **Alice Cooper**, **Aerosmith**, and **Kiss**, were all influenced by the British Glam Rock of **David Bowie** and **T.Rex**, who together pioneered the Glam Metal approach that would really take off in the 1980s with the advent of MTV.

Ritchie Blackmore left **Deep Purple** to form **Rainbow** with singer Ronnie James Dio. Other UK rockers like **Queen** and **Thin Lizzie** began to hit their stride. Meanwhile progressive rockers like **King Crimson** and **Van Der Graaf Generator** continued to push musical boundaries, even as some of their compatriots in **Yes** and **Genesis** arguably pushed boundaries of self indulgence.

In Europe, particularly in Germany, a new generation of bands such as **Can**, **Faust**, and **Kraftwerk** that was setting standards for later Alternative Rock, Avant-Garde, and Industrial Metal.

In the mid-1970s, beginning in New York and spreading to London, the New Wave and Punk Rock scenes were taking off, influenced by the noise rock of **The Velvet Underground** and the brutalism of **Iggy Pop and The Stooges**. Particularly worthy of mention are New York's **The Ramones**. Their minimalistic three-chord assault was a massive influence on subsequent Punk and Hardcore bands.

Meanwhile a fresh attitude to metal music was taking shape in the UK. A new generation of metal bands such as **Judas Priest**, **Iron Maiden**, **Saxon**, **Slayer**, **Def Leppard**, and **Motörhead** were fomenting their own movement: the New Wave of British Heavy Metal.

In the United States in the late 1970s Punk Rock was birthing Hardcore Punk, spearheaded by such bands as **The Dead Kennedys** and **Black Flag**. At the same time in Los Angeles Eddie Van Halen of **Van Halen** was pioneering a flashy new guitar technique. When the UK and US styles began to combine, the scene was set for the massive expansion of Heavy Metal music that was to occur worldwide in the 1980s, and continue on world-conquering to this day.

Kiss is a Fourth of July fireworks show with a backbeat

Gene Simmons of **KISS**

No American rock band has more gold albums than **Kiss**—28 in total. Who said Glam Metal didn't pay?

TIMELINE

1970

January
Black Sabbath release first album *Black Sabbath* on Friday 13th

May
King Crimson's second album, *In The Wake Of Poseidon*, released

June
Deep Purple's *Deep Purple In Rock* includes seminal track "Speed King"

July
The Stooges' *Fun House* is even more influential than their debut

August
Hawkwind release eponymous debut

September
Black Sabbath's *Paranoid* is the first Heavy Metal single to make #1

October
Led Zeppelin III is released

November
David Bowie's *The Man Who Sold The World* released

December
Marc Bolan's first album release as T.Rex—Glam Rock starts here

1971

January
Alice Cooper's *Love It to Death* takes rock theatricality to a new level

July
Black Sabbath's *Masters of Reality* is released

August
The Who release landmark production *Who's Next*

October
Deep Purple release *Fireball*

Van Der Graaf Generator release prog classic *Pawn Hearts* featuring Robert Fripp

November
Led Zeppelin release *Led Zeppelin IV*

1972

January
Blue Öyster Cult release their eponymous debut

March
Deep Purple release hit album *Machine Head*

Thin Lizzie release debut *Shades of a Blue Orphanage*

April
Wishbone Ash release sword 'n' sorcery classic *Argus*

May
Uriah Heep issue *Demons and Wizards*

June
Alice Cooper's "School's Out" is a smash hit

David Bowie's Ziggy Stardust unseats Bolan as Glam Rock king

Roxy Music's eponymous debut is another Alternative Rock blueprint

September
Black Sabbath's *Volume 4* released

Close To The Edge by Yes is a prog milestone

1973

January
Aerosmith's self-titled debut sets the scene for "Hair Metal"

Deep Purple release *Who Do We Think We Are*

February
The Stooges' *Raw Power* (produced by David Bowie) is another punk blueprint

March
Pink Floyd's *Dark Side of the Moon* raises production stakes

April
Queen's eponymous debut

July
Grand Funk Railroad pioneer stadium rock with *We're an American Band*

August
Lynyrd Skynyrd are kings of Southern Rock with platinum debut

December
Black Sabbath unleash *Sabbath Bloody Sabbath*

1974

February
Self-titled debut from **Kiss**—now face-painting!!

March
Rush release popular eponymous album

September
Judas Priest debut *Rocka Rolla*

October
King Crimson's *Red* is the last of their early albums

November
Queen's *Sheer Heart Attack* consolidates their style

1975

February
Aussie Rockers **AC/DC** debut album *High Voltage*

Led Zeppelin release *Physical Graffiti*

June
Ritchie Blackmore's Rainbow is released

October
Iron Butterfly release *Sun and Steel*, their last album of original material

November
A Night At The Opera is a huge smash for **Queen**

1976

March
Thin Lizzy's *Jailbreak* is their biggest seller

Kiss release multi-platinum album *Destroyer*

Judas Priest: *Sad Wings of Destiny*, often considered the start of the New Wave of British Heavy Metal

April
Rush release *2112*

The **Ramones** release eponymous debut, a vital blueprint for Punk and Hardcore and also an influence on the New Wave of British Heavy Metal.

May
Blue Öyster Cult's influential *Agents of Fortune*

Rising is second album from **Rainbow**

September
AC/DC release *Dirty Deeds Done Cheap*

Black Sabbath's *Technical Ecstacy*: the beginning of the end for singer Ozzy Osbourne

November
The **Sex Pistols'** debut single "Anarchy In The UK" officially kicks off the UK's Punk Rock movement

1977

March
AC/DC's *Let There Be Rock* issued in Australia

April
Judas Priest release *Sin After Sin*

August
Motörhead is unleashed!!

1978

February
Van Halen's eponymous debut

April
Rainbow release *Long Live Rock 'n' Roll*

May
AC/DC release *Powerage*

September
Kiss members each release self-titled solo albums

October
Judas Priest unleash *Killing Machine*

1979

January
Def Leppard release debut EP

March
Van Halen II is released
Motörhead second album *Overkill* issued

July
Rainbow release *Down To Earth*

August
Led Zeppelin are *In Through The Out Door*

October
Motörhead's *Bomber* takes off

November
The Soundhouse Tapes is **Iron Maiden's** debut EP

We love not just Judas Priest music, but we love heavy metal and we love to get out on that stage every night and perform. It's a joy to be able to do it.

Glenn Tipton

Above: L–R: Robert Plant, Jimmy Page, John Paul Jones, and John Bonham—**Led Zeppelin** performing on stage at the Bath Festival on June 28, 1970. While others may lay claim to the title of the first real Heavy Metal band, few of the pretenders have the credentials of Led Zeppelin whose muscular heavy blues gave way to riff-based hard rock.

Left: After starting as a session musician, Ritchie Blackmore went on to become one of the great guitarists with **Deep Purple** between 1968 and 1975. He left them to form **Rainbow** in 1975.

Above: The line-up of **Rainbow**—in New York in June 1975—
included, L–R: Gary Driscoll on drums, Micky Lee Soule on
keyboards, vocalist Ronnie James Dio, and
bassist Craig Gruber.

Above, Right: In 1974, Gary
Moore had replaced **Thin Lizzy's** original
guitarist, Eric Bell, but he was not to remain long. He left
soon after and later that year Brian Robertson (seen above with Phil
Lynott) took over. Moore came back as a temporary replacement for
Robertson in 1977. **Thin Lizzy** were mainly a hard rock act although
they strayed towards Heavy Metal.

Main Photo: The Blue Öyster Cult were one of the early American Heavy Metal acts. They are seen on stage at the Hammersmith Odeon in London in May 1978.

Above, Left: Lemmy— Ian Kilmister—and "Fast" Eddie Clarke (left) of **Motörhead.** One of the early Heavy Metal acts, **Motörhead** will always be remembered for "The Ace of Spades."

Above, Right: Alice Cooper has been performing since the mid-1960s, shocking many with his on-stage stunts and special effects. He hit the big time in the 1970s.

Above, Left: Black Sabbath—drums Bill Ward, guitar Tony Iommi, vocals Ozzy Osbourne, and bass Geezer Butler—were the most influential of the early Heavy Metal bands. From the pounding rain and tolling bell at the start of their first, eponymous, album they introduced the much-copied dark and demonic dimension to the music.

Above, Right: Shock Rock or—though they don't agree to the term—Glam Metal proponents Twisted Sister were an early 1970s band that finished in 1989 only to be reborn in 2003.

Above: Van Halen at the Palladium in New York in May 1979: L–R: Michael Anthony, Alex Van Halen (drums), David Lee Roth (vocals), Eddie Van Halen (lead guitar). Founded in the 1970s they would achieve their biggest sales in the 1980s.

Right: Gene Simmons of **Kiss.** In his demonic stage persona, he vomits artificial blood, spits out fire, and waggles his enormously long tongue.

Opposite: Another of the New Wave of British Heavy Metal, **Judas Priest** was formed in Birmingham in 1969. The key elements of the band were Rob Halford's operatic voice, twin guitars, and—latterly—leather and spikes.

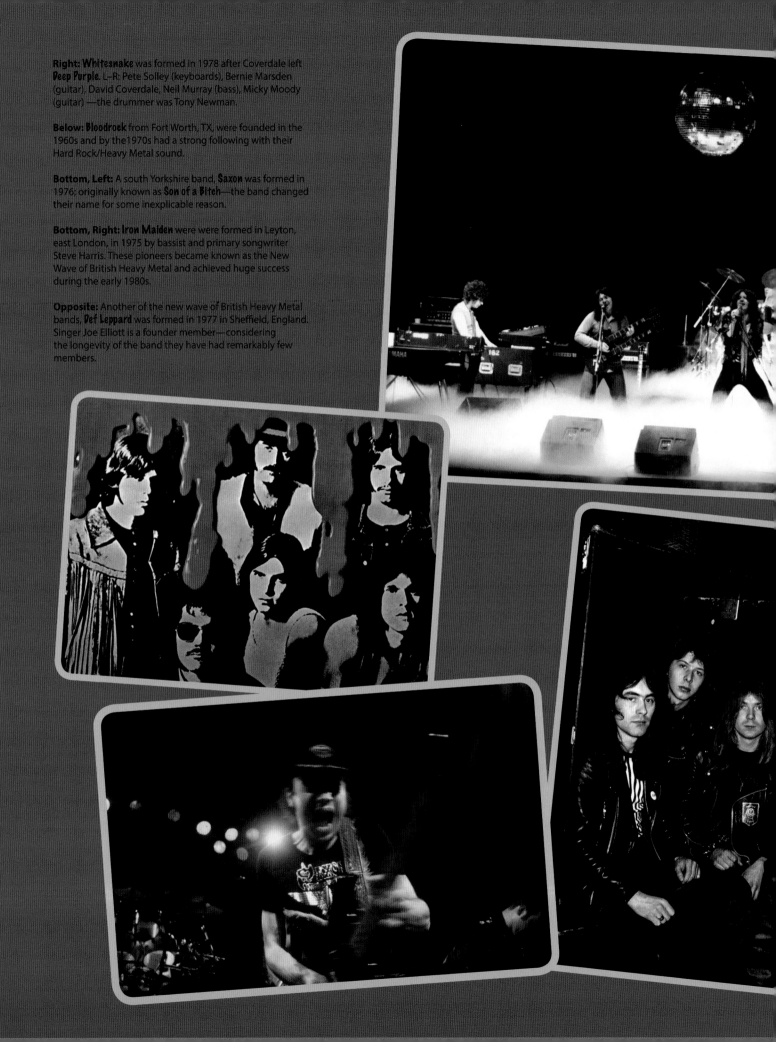

Right: Whitesnake was formed in 1978 after Coverdale left **Deep Purple**. L–R: Pete Solley (keyboards), Bernie Marsden (guitar), David Coverdale, Neil Murray (bass), Micky Moody (guitar) —the drummer was Tony Newman.

Below: Bloodrock from Fort Worth, TX, were founded in the 1960s and by the 1970s had a strong following with their Hard Rock/Heavy Metal sound.

Bottom, Left: A south Yorkshire band, **Saxon** was formed in 1976; originally known as **Son of a Bitch**—the band changed their name for some inexplicable reason.

Bottom, Right: Iron Maiden were were formed in Leyton, east London, in 1975 by bassist and primary songwriter Steve Harris. These pioneers became known as the New Wave of British Heavy Metal and achieved huge success during the early 1980s.

Opposite: Another of the new wave of British Heavy Metal bands, **Def Leppard** was formed in 1977 in Sheffield, England. Singer Joe Elliott is a founder member—considering the longevity of the band they have had remarkably few members.

3. THE 1980s

THE BIRTH OF METAL

It's an oft-repeated statistic: between 1983 and 1984 the market share of Heavy Metal music rose from 8% to 20%. A new generation was tiring of the synthesized arrangements of early 1980s Post Punk and New Romantic music. They were fed up with the arty pretentions of the New Wave. They wanted to get down and dirty, and the Hardcore Punk bands and New Wave of British Heavy Metal bands were serving up just the right musical cocktail.

At the same time, MTV was rewarding those bands who had the foresight to make promotional videos of their songs. One sector that particularly benefitted here was the Sunset Strip scene of Glam Metal bands such as **Mötley Crüe** and **Quiet Riot**. The UK bands caught on and **Def Leppard** really took off in the US after their video for "Pyromania" was aired. In the late 1980s, the MTV show *Headbanger's Ball* featured exclusively metal music. Inevitably though, there was a reaction against this polished and painted form of metal.

Thrash Metal, a stripped down and faster form of the music, was the earliest genre that was derived both from the Hardcore Punk of US bands such as **Black Flag** and UK bands like **Motörhead**. Four bands in particular epitomize it: **Anthrax**, **Slayer**, and the massively popular **Megadeth** and **Metallica**.

In 1986, **Slayer** released landmark album *Reign In Blood*. With its cleaner, tighter production and morbid thematic content, this album was to be highly influential on the emerging Death Metal scene.

Metal music became a wordwide phenomenon in the mid-1980s as bands from Germany (**Helloween**) to Brazil (**Sepultura**) came up with their own unique versions. Scandanavian bands like **Mercyful Fate** and **Bathory** perfected the Black Metal form. Sludge Metal from US northwest bands like **The Melvins** coalesced into Grunge.

Some vestiges of alternative rock crossed over into metal and were evident in the work of such bands as **Faith No More**, **The Red Hot Chile Peppers**, and **Jane's Addiction**.

Although some old guard bands such as **Led Zeppelin** and **Deep Purple** were no more, **Black Sabbath** and **Ozzy Osbourne** continued to be popular as separate entities, the former with new vocalist Ronnie James Dio and the latter with a successful solo career.

By the end of the 1980s, Metal music was truly a broad church. And in the following decade, the walls would only become broader and the congregation more diverse.

I can scare the pants off the holiest ghost.

Def Leppard

Formed by the Cavalera brothers Igor and Max in 1984, **Sepultura** is a Brazilian Thrash and Groove Metal band that found success in the late 1980s and early 1990s. When Max Cavalera left in 1998, he was replaced by Derrick Green.

TIMELINE

1980

February
UK band **Saxon** release popular album *Wheels Of Steel*

March
Def Leppard release debut album *On Through The Night*

April
Iron Maiden release eponymous debut album

Judas Priest release breakthrough album *British Steel*

July
AC/DC release *Back In Black*, their first after the death of original singer Bon Scott

September
Ozzy Osborne releases solo debut *The Blizzard of Ozz*

October
Killing Joke release self-titled debut, a big influence on subsequent Thrash Metal and Grunge

November
Motörhead's fourth album *Ace Of Spades* becomes their debut release in the USA

1981

February
Rainbow release fifth album *Difficult to Cure*

May
Canadian Speed Metal band **Anvil** debut *Hard 'n' Heavy*

September
King Crimson return from hiatus with *Discipline*

Bruce Dickinson replaces Paul Di'Anno as **Iron Maiden** vocalist

November
Mötley Crüe debut *Too Fast For Love* kicks off Glam Metal

1982

February
Mechanix is the most successful album for UK veterans **UFO**

March
Iron Maiden's *The Number of the Beast* is the first Heavy Metal album to hit #1 on the UK Album Chart

UK band **Diamond Head** release second album *Borrowed Time*

German band **Scorpions** release *Blackout*, including classic "China White"

April
Motörhead unleash *Iron Fist*

September
Twisted Sister decamp to the UK to record debut *Under The Blade*

November
Venom from Newcastle, England release influential album *Black Metal*

1983

July
Kill 'Em All is debut album from **Metallica**, kicking off Thrash Metal

September
Mötley Crüe release second album *Shout At The Devil*

Progressive Metal pioneers **Queensrÿche** issue self-titled debut EP

October
Danish band **Mercyful Fate** release influential debut album *Melissa*

November
Third solo album from **Ozzy Osbourne** is *Bark At The Moon*

December
Balls To The Wall is the fifth album from German band **Accept**

When I die, sprinkle my ashes over the '80's.

David Lee Roth of **Van Halen**

1984

July
Second album from **Metallica** is *Ride The Lightning*

September
Iron Maiden release *Powerslave*

Mercyful Fate release *Don't Break The Oath*

November
Morbid Tales is the debut album from influential Swiss band **Celtic Frost**

December
Def Leppard drummer Rick Allen loses his left arm in a car accident . . . but he's back within three months and the band goes from strength to strength

1985

March
Hell Awaits is second album from **Slayer**, one of the "big four" Thrash Metal bands

April
Bonded by Blood is the debut album from California Thrash Metal band **Exodus**

June
Megadeth (another "big four" Thrash Metal band) release debut album *Killing Is My Business…and Business Is Good!*

August
Metallica (kings of the "big four") play their biggest gig to date at Donington Park, England

October
Another of the "big four," **Anthrax** from New York City, release sophomore album *Spreading the Disease*

California's **Posessed** release debut *Seven Churches* and kick off Death Metal

1986

March
Metallica release third album *Master of Puppets*

June
Candlemass from Sweden release Doom Metal classic *Epicus Doomicus Metallicus*

September
Metallica tour bus crash kills bassist Cliff Burton

October
Sweden's **Bathory** release eponymous debut album, igniting Black Metal

Seattle's **Melvins** record *Gluey Porch Treatments*, a precursor of Sludge Metal and Grunge

November
Germany's **Kreator** release Thrash Metal classic *Pleasure To Kill*

1987

April
Californian Thrash Metal band **Testament** release debut album *The Legacy*

Voivod from Canada issue third album *Killing Technology*

May
Scream Bloody Gore by **Death** is a Death Metal classic

Keeper of the Seven Keys: Part 1 is the first album from German Power Metal band **Helloween**

Alternative Metal band **Jane's Addiction** release self-titled debut

July
Guns 'n' Roses, kings of the Sunset Strip scene, release debut *Appetite For Destruction*

Scum is the debut album of UK Grindcore band **Napalm Death**

October
Denmark's **King Diamond** release their first concept album *Abigail*

1988

May
Queensrÿche release their concept album *Operation Mindcrime*

August
Metallica hit the mainstream with fourth album … *And Justice For All*

October
Bathory expand their sound with *Blood Fire Death*, launching Viking Metal

1989

February
Flute-rock veterans **Jethro Tull** beat **Metallica** to win the first Grammy Award for Hard Rock / Heavy Metal

April
Canadian Thrash Metal band **Annihilator** release debut *Alice In Hell*

Brazilian Thrash Metal band **Sepultura** issue popular album *Beneath The Remains*

May
Tampa, Florida band **Morbid Angel** raise the Death Metal stakes with debut album *Altars of Madness*

June
King's X from Springfield, Missouri, anticipate Grunge and Groove Metal with debut album *Gretchen Goes to Nebraska*

Top, Left: South Yorkshire band, **Saxon** (L–R: singer Biff Byford, guitarist Graham Oliver, guitarist Paul Quinn, bassist Steve Dawson, and drummer Pete Gill), formed in 1976 and seen here in May 1979.

Top, Right: Playing and touring for 35 years **Iron Maiden** comprise L–R: Steve Harris, Nicko McBrain, Dave Murray, Adrian Smith, and Bruce Dickinson, seen performing onstage in September 1983.

Above and Opposite: Despite being one of the best selling bands in the world, **Mötley Crüe** planned to retire at the end of 2015. Nikki Sixx and Mick Mars onstage, and offstage, Nikki Sixx's bass guitars.

Right: Another British band founded in the 1970s that had a long and successful career is **Motörhead**. "Fast" Eddie Clarke and singer Ian "Lemmy" Kilmister on stage in July 2010 at the Norway Rock Festival. The latter died in 2015 and the band ceased to continue. Clarke died in January 2018.

Opposite: Ozzy Osbourne on April 18, 1984, at the Beverly Wilshire Hotel in Beverly Hills, CA. Ozzy resurrected his career after **Black Sabbath** as a solo artist.

Top: One of the first acts to fuse hardcore punk with Thrash Metal, the New York founded **Cro-Mags** became a seminal crossover act with their debut album *The Age of Quarrel*. They have had many changes of line-up, this was how they were in March 1987 at the Metro in Chicago, IL.

Left: After Ozzy left **Sabbath**, Ronnie James Dio (left) took over. He's seen here with Tony Iommi at the Oakland Coliseum in Oakland, CA on July 18, 1982.

Above, Right: Mathias Jabs with **The Scorpions** at the Oakland Coliseum in Oakland, California in July 1982. They formed in Hannover, Germany back in 1965 and are one of the best selling bands of all time.

Opposite: Axl Rose and Desi Craft of **Guns n' Roses** perform at the LA Street Scene on September 28, 1985, the year the band formed. Its first album, *Appetite for Destruction*, was released in 1987 and topped the *Billboard 200* in 1988—becoming the top-selling debut album in the US.

Left: Drummer Tico Torres of **Bon Jovi** performs on stage in Illinois in early March 1987. The previous year saw the release of their globally successful third album *Slippery When Wet*.

Below, Left: Axl Rose on stage at the Ritz Club.

Below: Canadian pioneering Hair Metal band **Anvil** on stage in the UK in 1983. They were the subject of a 2008 documentary movie made by their former roadie that considerably raised their profile.

I'm not God but if I were God, three-quarters of you would be girls, and the rest would be pizza and beer.

Axl Rose of **Guns N' Roses**

We're not changing our name.

Scott Ian of **Anthrax** after letters containing spores of lethal anthrax led to the death of five people.

Opposite, Above: **Slayer** was founded in 1981 in California. One of the "Big Four" of Thrash Metal (with **Metallica**, **Anthrax**, and **Megadeth**). They have received five Grammy nominations despite their controversial (to the mainstream) themes of Satanism, necrophilia, and other nihilistic pursuits.

Opposite, Below Left: Lead singer of the flashy Glam Metal band **Ratt**, Stephen Pearcy, prances on stage during a 1987 Long Beach, CA, concert at the Long Beach Arena.

Opposite, Below Right: Trey Azagthoth of **Morbid Angel.** The band was one of the founders of Death Metal and Azagthoth is rated by many as the number one Death Metal guitarist.

Right: Dan Spitz of Heavy Metal band **Anthrax** performs on stage at the Monsters of Rock Festival held at Donington Park on August 22, 1987.

> The '80s
> were the
> worst
> period. You
> had these
> horrible
> pop bands
> growing
> their hair
> and calling
> themselves
> metal.

Geezer Butler of
Black Sabbath

Opposite: Glam Metal **Warrant** hail from Hollywood, CA. They have had frequent changes of personnel: this is the line up for the "Under the Influence" tour in 2001.

Above: Australian hard rockers **AC/DC** were founded by brothers Angus (above in Sacramento, in June 1988) and Malcolm Young in Sydney in 1973; since then they have sold over 200 million albums worldwide.

Below: Chuck Schuldiner was founder and leader of pioneering Death Metal band **Death**. He is seen here in New York City in February 1995. Schuldiner is often referred to as the "Father of Death Metal" following the success of their first album *Scream Bloody Gore*. The band folded when Schuldiner died of brain cancer in December 2001.

HEAVY METAL THE STORY IN PICTURES

Opposite, Above: German thrash metal band **Kreator** formed in 1982 but had to wait until the 1990s to achieve recognition. Seen here live at Tuska Open Air 2013.

Opposite, Below: Thrash Metal **Megadeth** in 1988. Their lyrics feature themes of death, politics, war, and religion set to fast and complex rhythms. This has made them at times a controversial band and seen some of their work banned.

Above: Jane's Addiction at Big Day Out, Melbourne, Australia in January 2003. They have dissolved and reformed four times. In the early 1990s, they were the first alternative rock band to gain mainstream acceptance and success in the US, and became leaders of the self-dubbed "Alternative Nation."

Right: Timo Kotipelto of Finnish Power metal band **Stratovarius.** Formed in 1984, they have released sixteen studio albums, four DVDs, and five live albums. They are considered one of the leading and most influential groups of the Power Metal genre alongside German bands **Helloween, Blind Guardian**, and **Gamma Ray.**

Main Photo: Bassist Jason Newsted and singer/guitarist James Hetfield of **Metallica** perform onstage at the Monsters of Rock festival at Rice Stadium on July 2, 1988 in Houston, TX.

Below: Metallica formed as a Thrash Metal band in Los Angeles in 1981. After a slow start playing only to afficianados, the band became popular to a much wider audience after 1991 to become one of the most commercially successful bands of all time. Here, James Hetfield is shown at the Rock in Rio Festival in September 2013.

Bottom: Metallica at Aardshock Festival. Now with their own record label (Blackened) and Detroit music festival (Orion Music + More), Metallica may be more mainstream than they were in 1980s but they are still influential Heavy Metal beasts.

There is one Metallica. We have many styles, it's called Metallica.

James Hetfield

4. THE 1990s

METAL SPLINTERS

At the beginning of the 1990s, Glam Metal and Thrash Metal still reigned supreme. Thrash leaders **Metallica** were enjoying massive sales. The tougher end of the Sunset Strip scene was personified by **Guns 'n' Roses**. Death and Black Metal were still largely underground.

Then came the howl from the Pacific Northwest commonly referred to as the Grunge movement. Bands like **Nirvana** and **Soundgarden** brought a new immediacy but also a new level of melodic content to their material. They were reacting against the commerciality of Hair Metal but ironically, they often were just as commercially successful, if not more so, than the bands they reacted against. In the case of Kurt Cobain of **Nirvana** the stress of international fame probably contributed to his tragic suicide in 1994.

A similar movement was occurring in the Southern California desert where Stoner Rock band **Kyuss** later begat **Queens of the Stone Age**.

Perry Farrell of **Jane's Addiction** launched the touring festival Lollapalooza in 1991. A few years later, the godfather of Metal, Ozzy Osbourne, launched his own version, Ozzfest. Many young metal acts would be broken in at these festivals.

In Norway, the Black Metal scene was developing in its own way. Never was a band more aptly named than **Mayhem**, with its history of murder and suicide. However, behind the sensational headlines some serious musical skills were being brought to an ever more complex genre. In the States, Death and Doom Metal were taken to new heights, or depths, by bands such as **Death** and **Cannibal Corpse**.

Germany's Power Metal bands such as **Helloween** brought blinding musicianship combined with an epic helping of sword and sorcery-inspired sagas.

The early Funk Metal experiments of bands like **Red Hot Chile Peppers** and **Faith No More** evolved into the Alternative and Rap Metal of **Rage Against the Machine** and **System of a Down**. As the decade progressed these styles coalesced into the Nu Metal of **Korn** and **Limp Bizkit**.

The Groove Metal genre of bands was exemplified by the likes of **Pantera** and **Machine Head**, utilizing slower tempos (but not Doom or Sludge Metal slow).

"Industrial" elements began to be incorporated with great success by the likes of **Fear Factory**, **Marilyn Manson**, and Germany's **Rammstein**.

By the turn of the century, Heavy Metal had become so diverse that that the term was arguably meaningless.

> Anthrax, it's something that gets you sick, it's horrible, strong. It's a heavy-metal band name if there ever was one.
>
> Scott Ian

Extreme Metal **Mayhem** came screaming and raging out of Norway in the early 1980s. They became notorious for their violent and chaotic public and private lives, nevertheless, they are one of the most influential bands in their genre.

TIMELINE

April
Thrash Metal band **Death Angel** from California release third album *Act III*

June
Swedish Death Metal band **Entombed** release debut album *Left Hand Path*

Florida Black Metal band **Deicide** release eponymous debut

July
Cowboys From Hell is the first major label album from **Pantera**

September
Megadeth release fourth album *Rust In Peace*

January
Def Leppard guitarist Steve Clark dies from a mixture of prescription drugs and alcohol.

April
Per Yngve Ohlin (aka "Dead"), vocalist for Norwegian Black Metal **Mayhem** commits suicide

July
Metallica's "black album" goes multi-platinum

Perry Farrell of Alternative Rock band **Jane's Addiction** launches first Lollapalooza touring festival

September
Palm Desert, California band **Kyuss** pioneer Stoner Rock with their debut album *Wretch*

October
Death release Death Metal classic *Human*

Nevermind from Seattle's **Nirvana** brings the Grunge movement to worldwide attention

November
Freddie Mercury of **Queen** dies

February
Los Angeles band **Tool** release debut album *Undertow*

Pantera perfect their Groove Metal style with sixth album *Vulgar Display Of Power*

Def Leppard recruit Vivian Campbell as a replacement for Steve Clark

July
Boston's **Dream Theater** release their bestseller *Images and Words*

September
Buffalo band **Cannibal Corpse** issue controversial album *Tomb of the Mutilated*

Alice In Chains release Grunge hit *Dirt*

November
Eponymous debut album from **Rage Against The Machine** released

April
Florida's **Savatage** release seventh album *Edge of Thorns*; soon after, guitarist Criss Oliva is killed by a drunk driver

August
Øystein Aarseth, guitarist for **Mayhem**, is murdered by bassist Varg Vikernes

October
Liverpool Grindcore band **Carcass** release breakthrough album *Heartwork*

Brooklyn's **Life of Agony** release debut *River Runs Red*

February
Norwegian Black Metal band **Emperor** release landmark album *In the Nightside Eclipse*, incorporating symphonic elements

March
Seattle Grunge gods **Soundgarden** release breakthrough album *Superunknown*

April
Nirvana singer and songwriter Kurt Cobain commits suicide

July
Marilyn Manson debut album is *Portrait of an American Family*

August
Californian Groove Metal band **Machine Head** issue debut album *Burn My Eyes*

October
Bakersfield, California band **Korn** release their eponymous debut, kicking off Nu Metal

1995

April
Finnish Power Metal band **Stratovarius** release fourth album *Fourth Dimension*

May
German Power Metal band **Gamma Ray** release fourth album *Land of the Free*

June
Fear Factory from Los Angeles pioneer Industrial Metal with their album *Demanufacture*

July
German Thrash Metal band **Kreator** incorporate some Industrial elements on their album *Cause for Conflict*

1996

January
Chicago Industrial Metal band **Ministry** release highest charting album *Filth Pig*

April
Evil Empire by **Rage Against The Machine** enters Billboard 200 at #1

Oakland's **Neurosis** release Avant-Garde Metal classic *Through Silver In Blood*

June
Metallica issue sixth album *Load*

Swedish Progressive Metal band **Opeth** release acclaimed sophomore album *Morningrise*

August
Swedish Symphonic Metal band **Therion** release *Theli*, featuring two choirs

September
Tool release second album *Ænima*, which enters Billboard 200 at #2

October
Ozzy Osbourne launches touring festival Ozzfest after being rejected by Lollapalooza

1997

April
Stratovarius release concept album *Visions*

June
Swedish Power Metal band **HammerFall** release debut album *Glory to the Brave*

July
Florida's **Limp Bizkit** release debut album *Three Dollar Bill, Y'all*

August
German Industrial Metal band **Rammstein** release sophomore album *Sehnsucht*

November
Finland's **Children of Bodom** release melodic Black Metal classic *Something Wild*

1998

February
Swedish melodic Death Metal band **Amon Amarth** release debut album *Once Sent from the Golden Hall*

March
Fourteenth album from **Motörhead** is *Snake Bite Love*

April
German Power Metal masters **Blind Guardian** release Tolkien-inspired *Nightfall in Middle Earth*

June
System of a Down unleash eponymous debut

August
Hellbilly Deluxe from **Rob Zombie** blends metal, pop, and electronics

September
Self-titled debut album from desert rockers **Queens of the Stone Age** unleashed

Mechanical Animals is a #1 album for **Marilyn Manson**

1999

January
Seattle Progressive Metal band **Nevermore** release acclaimed album *Dreaming Neon Black*

Singer Bruce Dickinson returns to **Iron Maiden**

March
M3 is third album from Industrial Metal band **Mushroomhead** from Cleveland, Ohio

June
Limp Bizkit hit #1 with sophomore album *Significant Other*

Slipknot release self-titled debut

August
Long Island Metalcore band **Vision of Disorder** issue album *For The Bleeders*

October
Opeth release anti-Christian concept album *Still Life*

Rage Against The Machine release *The Battle of Los Angeles*

Main Photo and Right: *Amorphis* formed in Finland in 1990 as a Death Metal band, but later moved stylistically into other metal genres. Here, Tomi Joutsen performs at Bloodstock Open Air Metal Festival in August 2010.

Below: Heavy Metal female rockers *Phantom Blue* formed in Los Angeles in 1987 and are shown here in the 1990s. They enjoyed some success, but after many personnel changes, broke up in 2001. They reformed in 2009.

Opposite: Controversial cult Death Metal band **Cannibal Corpse** explore the horror genre in lyrics and imagery. Here George "Corpsegrinder" Fisher performs at Shoreline Amphitheatre on July 29, 2006 in Mountain View CA.

Right: Loud and fast **Sepultura** (Portuguese for "grave") hail from Belo Horizonte, Brazil. They were one of the most important Heavy Metal bands of the 1990s.

Below: Controversial founder and leader Kristian—better known as Varg—Vikernes of Norwegian Black Metal band **Burzum** (which means "Darkness" in J.R.R. Tolkein's fictional Black language). Although hugely influential, Vikernes has never played live: in May 1994 he was sentenced to 21 years for the murder of his guitarist and arson. After releasing two albums in prison, since his release in 2009 he has recorded four more albums.

Below, Right: Kita, drummer for **Lordi**, which formed in Rovaniemi, Finland, in 1996. They are known for their pyrotechnics and monster masks and are the only Hard Rock act to win the Eurovision Song Contest (in 2006). Seen here at Download Festival in June 2005 in Leicestershire, England.

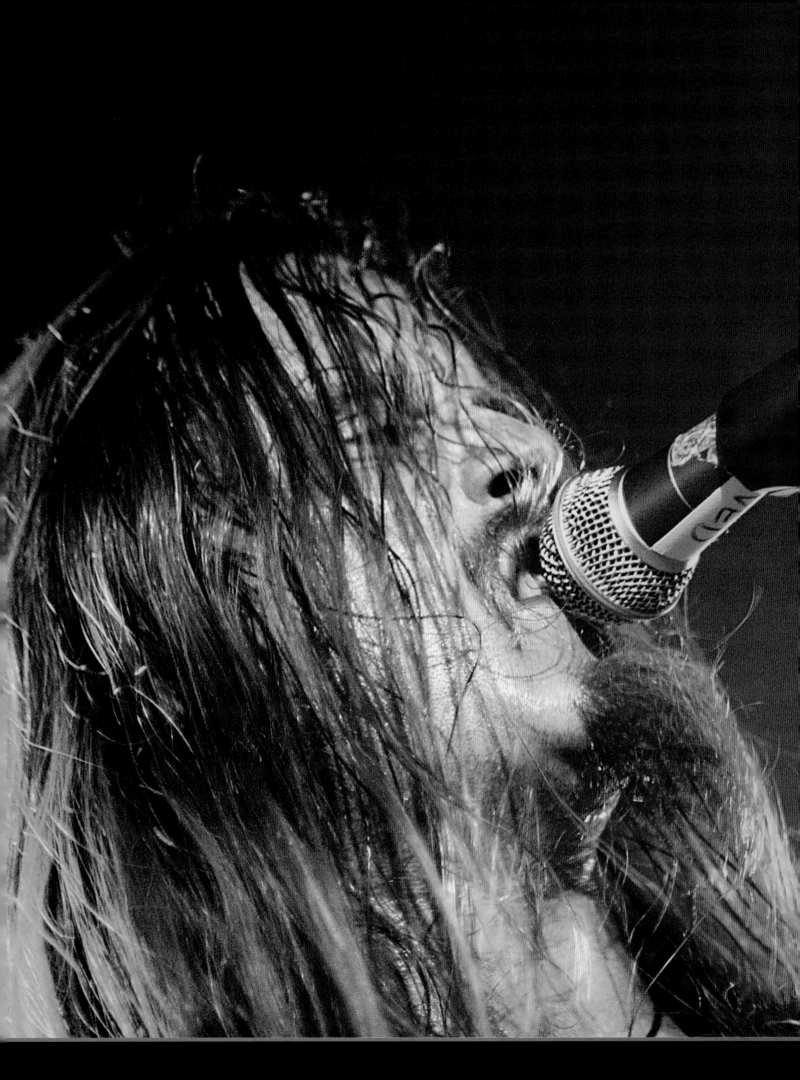

Main Photo: Norwegian Black/Viking Metal band **Enslaved** formed in 1991. Founder member Grutle Kjellson (lead vocals and bass) seen in 2006.

Below: Former rapper Ice-T formed **Body Count** in 1990 with old school friends. Their work references social and political issues and became notorious through the single "Cop Killer." On stage at White River Amphitheater in July 2014 in Auburn, Washington.

Bottom: Swedish Heavy Metal outfit **Europe** in New York in 1991. L–R: Mic Michaeli, Ian Haugland, John Leven, Kee Marcello, and Joey Tempest.

Main Photo: Shock (shlock?) rocker **Alice Cooper** in concert, 1991.

Right: Ice T fronting **Body Count** at the Hollywood Palladium on October 16, 1992 in Los Angeles, CA.

Below: New Wave US Groove/Thrash Metal **Machine Head** formed in 1991. They have explored various metal genres over the years and have become more rhythmically complex, heavier, and faster.

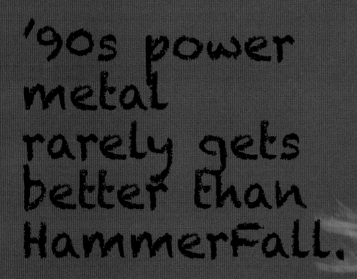

'90s power metal rarely gets better than HammerFall.

Jason Anderson, Allmusic

Main Photo: Oscar Dronjak, left, and Fredrik Larsson of Power Metal **HammerFall** (founded Gothenburg, Sweden in 1993). Festival favorites, the band has had many changes of line-up. Photographed at High Voltage Festival in London, July, 2010.

Opposite, Above: Initially labeled Nu Metal, **Kittie** formed as an all-female band in 1996 and have altered their style to be variously described as Alternative or Extreme Metal. Here touring debut album *Spit* at Ozzfest 2000.

Opposite, Center: Korey Cooper of **Skillet** (formed 1996), the hard-touring Christian Metal band from Memphis. May 2010.

Opposite, Below: Gaahl, the singer with Black Metal band **Gorgoroth**. Founded in Sunnfjord in Norway in 1992, they are an openly Satanist band and are now based in Bergen. Their seminal album *Under The Sign Of Hell* came out in 1997.

Main Photo: Tobias Sammet of Power Metal **Edguy** (founded 1992 in Fulda, Germany). They reject pedaling any religious or political message preferring a wider based vision for their music which can include humor and, on occasion, an orchestra. Here at Olympiahalle, Munich in May 2010.

Opposite, Above: Shinya of the Japanese Metal band **Dir En Grey** (formed 1997 in Osaka). Hard to classify and with ever-changing styles, the band now is generally labeled as Progressive Metal. Shown in Moscow in August 2011.

Opposite, Below: Barry Stock of Canadian **Three Days Grace** (formed 1997) performs their Alternative Metal music in January 2005 in Miami, FL.

Dark Funeral is the shit!

Joey Jordison, **Slipknot**

Opposite, Above: Mudvayne (formed Peoria, IL, 1996). Variously described as belonging to multiple metal genres, they jokingly referred to themselves as Math Metal, alluding to the complexity of their music. They have been on hiatus since 2010.

Opposite, Below: Magnus Broberg of Swedish Black Metal outfit Dark Funeral (founded 1993) at Bloodstock 2013. Satanism is a strong theme in the band with many of the (changing) personnel being practicing Satanists.

Below, Left: Drummer Mike Wengren of Disturbed (founded Chicago, 1997), touring their debut album *The Sickness* in 2001. They were hugely successful in the years around the millennium but went on indefinite hiatus in 2011, although they have every intention of reforming.

Below, Right: Lead singer Josh Todd of US Heavy Metal Buckcherry (formed 1995). Their eponymous first album (1999) contained a couple of crossover hits and went gold.

Above: Sully Erna (left) and Tony Rambola (right) of Alternative Metal **Godsmack** (formed 1995 in Lawrence, MA) in June 2000. Their success had led to the mayor of Boston declaring August 6 "Godsmack Day."

Above, Right: Finnish Folk Metal band **Korpiklaani**—"Forest Clan" in Finnish—formed in Lahti in 1993 when they were known as **Shaman**. Alongside electric guitars they also use traditional folk instruments and often sing about nature.

Right: L–R: bassist Reginald "Fieldy" Arvizu, singer and bagpipe player Jonathan Davis, and guitarist and backing vocalist James "Munky" Shaffer of Nu Metal **Korn** (formed 1993, Bakersfield, CA). Their themes are personal alienation and pain. April 1995 in New York City.

Opposite: Sharon den Adel and Robert Westerholt—joint founders of **Within Temptation** (formed 1996, Waddinxveen, Netherlands)—in May 2007 at the Pinkpop Festival. Originally playing Gothic Metal they moved on to exploring Symphonic Metal, plus a wide range of styles between.

Above: Arch Enemy are a group of experienced musicians from other metal bands. They play Melodic Death Metal (formed Halmstad, Sweden, 1996).

Right: Vocalist Elias Soriano of Nu Metal **Nonpoint** (formed Fort Lauderdale, FL, 1997) in May 2001.

Below: Notable for their electric violin solos, **Turisas** (formed Hämeenlinna, Finland, 1997) play Finnish Folk Metal. Shown in July 2006 at Bloodstock.

Opposite, Above: Jamey Jasta of **Hatebreed** (formed Bridgepost, CT, 1994) play Crossover Thrash with Hardcore Punk. Seen at Leeds Festival in August 2010.

Opposite, Below: The precise musical genre of Finland's **Children of Bodom** (founded Espoo, Finland, in 1993) is hotly debated by fans and critics—lead guitarist and vocalist Alexi Laiho calls it Extreme Metal, since all the other alternatives are too restrictive.

Main Photo: Another view of Mr. Lordi (Tomi Petteri Putaansuu) who designs and makes all the masks and costumes for his band **Lordi**. He also designs the sets and all the graphics. The band struggled in the 1990s before signing a deal with Bertelsmann in 2002.

Below: Top Death Metal band **Deicide** in 1995, the year their third album, *Once Upon the Cross*, came out. Short at twenty-eight minutes long, it was even shorter when played in concert.

Bottom: **Static X** (formed 1994) played Industrial Metal and Nu Metal but folded in 2013: it was reported that Wayne Static (featured here) died the following year.

Opposite, Above: Canadian rockers **Voivod** started out as a Speed Metal outfit but have developed their own Thrash/Progressive Metal style. Here touring *The Outer Limits* in January 1994.

Opposite, Below: Heavy Metal **Mushroomhead** have had many changes of line-up. Their music combines many and varied metal styles. They formed in 1993.

Above: Soulfly in 2003 at the Elserhalle. Formed by Max Cavalera, former front man of **Sepultura**, they play world music and Brazilian-inspired metal.

Right: Erik Rutan of US Death Metal/Extreme Metal **Hate Eternal** sing about domination and the heroes and villans of long ago.

Below: US Black Metal band **Kult ov Azazel** (formed 1998) co-headlining at home (with **Cannibal Corpse**) in Fort Lauderdale, FL, in January 2012.

Bottom, Left: Marduk is a Black Metal band from Norrköping, Sweden. The band formed in 1990 and released their first record in 1991.

Bottom, Right: Vinnie Stigma of **Agnostic Front** seen in 1998. Labeled Crossover Thrash, the band emerged from the New York Hardcore scene in the mid-1980s.

Opposite, Above: Daniel Jacobs (L) and Marc McKnight of Metalcore/Alternative Metal **Atreyu** (formed 1998). After heavy touring the band members took a break in 2011 while they pursued individual side projects. They reformed in 2014 with new music and live gigs.

Opposite, Below: Daniel Varghamne (R) and Niklas Isfeldt of Swedish Heavy Metal **Dream Evil**. Set up in 1999 by producer Fredrik Nordström; seen here on stage at Hammerfest, March 2012.

We all break down, we all stop as the line between machinery and humanity blurs.

Atreyu

Main Photo: The **Scorpions** formed in Hannover, Germany in 1965 and are still playing—they celebrated their 50th anniversary in March 2015. They claim sales of over 100 million records; their biggest global hit is their 1980s Heavy Metal anthem "Rock You Like A Hurricane." Seen here at Zenith in Paris, in May 1999.

Below: Brandan Schieppati and **Bleeding Through** (formed in Orange County, CA, 1999). Usually labeled Metalcore, Schieppati disagrees and considered them a Hardcore band. Shown here in 2008 at Download. After announcing their final tour, they played their last gig on August 3, 2014.

Opposite, Inset: Aaron Stainthorpe of **My Dying Bride** on stage at Hellfire Festival at NEC Arena in November 2009 in Birmingham, England. They formed as a Doom Metal band in Bradford, England in 1990.

We're all hardcore kids and we came from the hardcore scene.

Brandan Schieppati of
Bleeding Through

Main Photo: Tobias Sammet, former singer for **Edguy**, now founder of German Progressive Metal supergroup **Avantasia**. The band is Sammet's intermittent Metal Opera project which started in 1999, featuring the participation of guest musicians. Shown here in Sweden in June 2013. The final performance took place at the Wacken Festival in Germany in August 2014.

Above: Warrel Dane and **Nevermore** (co-headlining with **Symphony X**) at Elysee Montmartre on February 28, 2011 in Paris, France, a few weeks before the tour ended. **Nevermore** then went into abeyance, twenty years after they were founded in Seattle.

5. THE 2000s

METAL FOR THE NEW MILLENNIUM

For an industry that relies on the technological savvy of its artists, the music business has always been suspicious of new technology and slow to adopt it. In the case of the Internet revolution at the turn of the century, the record companies and music publishers gave the whole thing away. They were asleep at the wheel while certain huge corporations and various nameless pirates cornered and stole the whole thing from under them.

Not that this in any way hampered the relentless burgeoning of Metal Music. The collapse of physical recorded media only put more emphasis on live performance. The scene could hardly be more vibrant.

In the 2000s, Metalcore emerged as a commercial force with bands such as **Converge** and **Killswitch Engage** making inroads on the Billboard 200. Metalcore evolved into Mathcore as such bands as **The Dillinger Escape Plan** made ever more technical and demanding music. Southern California's **Avenged Sevenfold** evolved beyond their Metalcore roots and became one of the most commercially successful Metal bands of the new century thus far.

A new genre known as Deathcore began to emerge, with bands like **Whitechapel** and **The Acacia Strain** embracing the mix of Death Metal with Metalcore and Hardcore Punk. Meanwhile Chicago's **Disturbed** kept the Nu Metal flag flying.

Black Metal continued to evolve closer to the mainstream. Norway's **Dimmu Borgir** and **Satyricon**, and the UK's **Cradle of Filth** released successful albums.

A certain category of bands is often dubbed "Retro Metal" for their adherence to the precepts of early metal pioneers such as **Black Sabbath** and **Deep Purple**. Bands of this type include California's **High On Fire** and Sweden's **Witchcraft**.

The old guard themselves were hardly absent. **Saxon**, **Judas Priest**, **Iron Maiden**, **Deep Purple,** and **King Crimson** all released albums during the first decade of the new century. Meanwhile, the Thrash Metal upstarts of the early 1980s were still going strong. **Metallica**, **Megadeth**, and **Slayer** all released successful albums during this period.

Glam Metal may have gone out of style, but comedy band **Steel Panther** kept the flame burning. The original glam guys were still around: **Bon Jovi** went country, **Mötley Crüe** and **Ratt** reformed. UK band **The Darkness** got a lot of attention with their 2003 debut *Permission To Land*.

So, as the traditional core of metal was nurtured and strengthened, bands on the fringes of the movement continued to push the boundaries and try different blends. This trend would continue into the next decade.

Opposite, Above: L–R: Troy Sanders, Bill Kelliher, Brann Dailor, Brent Hinds of **Mastodon**—formed in 2000, they would develop into one of the top metal acts of the new millennium.

Opposite, Below: Nick Hipa and vocalist Tim Lambesis of Metalcore **As I Lay Dying** at Bloodstock. Since February 2014, Lambesis has been serving six years for solicitation of murder. The band is on hiatus: the other members instead have formed **Wovenwar**.

A kid once said to me "Do you get hangovers?" I said, "To get hangovers you have to stop drinking."

Lemmy,
Motörhead

TIMELINE

2000

March
Dio release *Magica*

June
Mayhem survive the carnage and release second album *Grand Declaration of War*

Seattle Avant-Garde Metal outfit Sunn O))) release first album *ØØ Void*

July
Swedish Death Metal band In Flames release fifth album *Clayman*

September
Virginia Groove Metal band Lamb of God release sophomore album *New American Gospel*

October
Cradle of Filth release fourth album *Midian*

Linkin Park from California hit #2 on the *Billboard 200* with debut album *Hybrid Theory*

2001

February
Opeth consolidate their style with *Blackwater Park*

May
Staind get through to mass appeal with third album *Break the Cycle*

Tool make a triumphant return with *Lateralus*

August
Slipknot release successful second album *Iowa*

September
God Hates Us All by Slayer is released on 9/11

Saxon release fifteenth album *Killing Ground*

System of a Down release big hit album *Toxicity*

2002

March
Soilwork from Sweden release fourth album *Natural Born Chaos*

April
German Power Metal band Primal Fear release first concept album *Black Sun*

August
Portland Folk Metal band Agalloch release second album *The Mantle*

2002

September
The UK's Porcupine Tree release second album *In Absentia*

November
Debut album from Audioslave makes #7 on *Billboard 200*, features former Rage Against the Machine members with former Soundgarden singer Chris Cornell

2003

March
Thirteenth album from King Crimson is *The Power to Believe*

April
US Alternative Metal band Godsmack hit *Billboard 200* #1 with third album *Faceless*

May
The Golden Age of Grotesque is another #1 for Marilyn Manson

June
Metallica release eighth album *St Anger*

July
Rob Halford rejoins Judas Priest

September
Iron Maiden issue their thirteenth album *Dance of Death*

October
Florida's Trivium release debut *Ember to Inferno*

2004

January
Florida's Iced Earth release concept album *The Glorious Burden*

May
The End of Heartache is a gold album for Massachusetts Metalcore band Killswitch Engage

August
Mastodon issue Sludge Metal classic *Leviathan*

November
Dutch Symphonic Metal band Within Temptation release third album *The Silent Force*

2005

December
Former **Pantera** guitarist Dimebag Darrell is murdered on stage in Ohio

February
Judas Priest come back with *Angel of Retribution*

June
Southern California's **Avenged Sevenfold** move on from Metalcore with third album *City of Evil*

July
Swedish Death Metal band **Arch Enemy** release sixth album *Doomsday Machine*

August
Opeth masterpiece *Ghost Reveries* adds keyboards

September
New Jersey's **God Forbid** release *IV:Constitution of Treason*

October
Exodus release seventh album *Shovel Headed Kill Machine*

2006

March
Sepultura release tenth album *Dante XXI*

April
Swedish Progressive Metal band **Evergrey** release sixth album *Monday Morning Apocalypse*

Norwegian Black Metal band **Satyricon** release grooving sixth album *Now, Diabolical*

May
Tool return to #1 with the masterful *10,000 Days*

June
Christian Metal band **Underoath** hit #2 on the *Billboard 200* with fifth album *Define the Great Line*

August
Sacrament by **Lamb of God** debuts at #8 on the *Billboard 200*

September
Third album from **Mastodon** is the more melodic *Blood Mountain*

Amon Amarth release sixth album *With Oden on Our Side*

October
Hammerfall release sixth album *Threshold*

2007

April
Mayhem return with fourth album *Ordo Ad Chao*

May
Megadeth release eleventh album *United Abominations*

June
Groove Metal band **DevilDriver** release second album *The Fury of Our Maker's Hand*

September
Sweden's **Arch Enemy** release seventh album *Rise of the Tyrant*

November
New Jersey Mathcore band **The Dillinger Escape Plan** release third album *Ire Works*

2008

January
Welsh Metalcore outfit **Bullet For My Valentine** release second album *Scream Aim Fire*

March
Swedish Avant-Garde Metal band **Meshuggah** release sixth album *obZen*

April
Children of Bodom are #1 in Finland with *Blooddrunk*

August
All Hope Is Gone is platinum fourth album for **Slipknot**

September
Trivium release fourth album *Shogun*

Metallica return with *Death Magnetic*

October
AC/DC come back with fifteenth album *Black Ice*

2009

February
Lamb of God release sixth album *Wrath*

March
Fourth album from **Mastodon** is *Crack the Skye*

April
The Dio version of **Black Sabbath** reunites as **Heaven and Hell**, releases hit album *The Devil You Know*

August
Poland's **Behemoth** issue *Evangelion*

October
Massachusetts Metalcore band **Converge** release seventh album *Axe To Fall*

November
Slayer return reinvigorated with *World Painted Blood*

Above: Joakim Broden (L) and Par Sundstrom of Swedish Power Metal band **Sabaton**. Formed in the late 1990s, they sing of historical battles and warfare. They produced their first album, *Primo Victoria*, in 2005. Thanks to relentless touring, in April 2012 four members left the band wanting to spend more time at home. This is the new line-up in June 2011 at the *Metal Hammer* Golden Gods Awards.

Right: US Alternative Rock band **A Perfect Circle**—lead vocalist Maynard James Keenan, guitarist Troy Van Leeuwen, bassist/violinist Paz Lenchantin, drummer Josh Freese, and lead guitarist Billy Howerdel—released three albums 2000–2004 before a six-year hiatus. They reformed to tour again in 2010.

Below, Right: Elias Viljanen and Henrik Klingenberg of Finnish Power Metal band **Sonata Arctica** (formed 1995 as rock band **Tricky Beans**), although they prefer to label themselves Melodic Metal. Their most successful album, *Reckoning Night*, was released in 2004; helped by a North American tour supporting **Nightwish**, *Reckoning Night* was certified Gold in Finland in February 2006 and the band's website says it has gone on to sell 100,000 copies worldwide.

Opposite: Luke Hoskin of Canadian Progressive Metal band **Protest the Hero**. Their first release was EP *Search for the Truth*, in 2002, but it was their second album, *Fortress* (2008), that saw them hit the big time as it peaked at #1 in the Canadian charts.

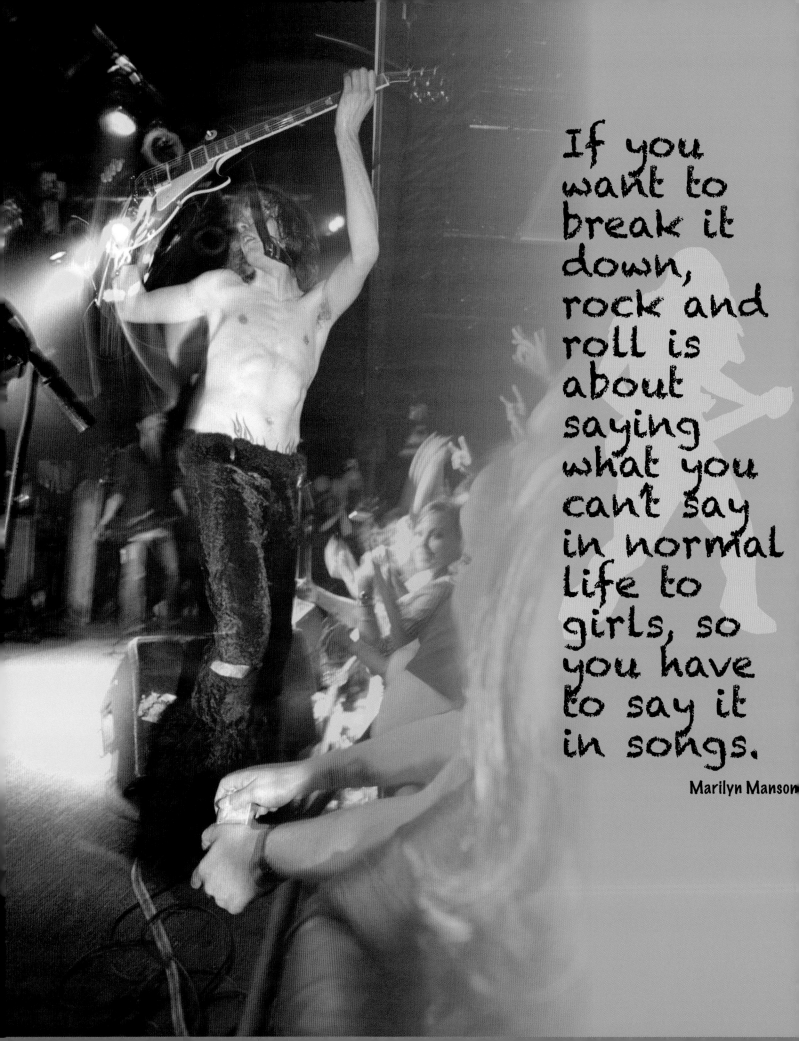

If you want to break it down, rock and roll is about saying what you cant say in normal life to girls, so you have to say it in songs.

Marilyn Manson

Opposite: Justin Hawkins of **The Darkness** performing at the Metro club, London 2003. Their debut album *Permission to Land* reached #1 in the British charts but after huge success, the Glam Metal band went on hiatus between 2006 and 2011 when they reformed.

Left: Andreas Bergh of Swedish Gothic Metal band **Deathstars** in 2007. They perform with face paint and Gothic attire and sing songs of horror and misanthropy.

Below: L–R: Matt Caughthran, Jorma Vik, and Brad Magers of Hardcore Punk LA band **The Bronx.** They have released four studio albums and three more mariachi music albums as *Mariachi El Bronx.*

Above: German Power Metal **Powerwolf** in Berlin in 2013 without their corpse paint. Formed in 2002 they sing songs of vampires and werewolves and other gothic-inspired tales.

Right: Guitarist Nick Piunno and singer Johnathan "Johnny Plague" Cooke of Californian band **Winds of Plague** (originally formed in 2002 as **Bleak December**). They are one of the very few Deathcore bands to incorporate symphonic elements in their music.

Below: Hernan "Eddie" Hermida of Deathcore **Suicide Silence** in July 2014. He replaced Mitch Lucker as lead vocalist after the latter died in a motorbike wreck in late 2012. Their brilliant debut album, *The Cleansing*, appeared in 2007.

Right: Bobby "Blitz" Ellsworth of East Coast Thrash Metal **Overkill** in 2000. The band's mascot is a green-eyed skeletal bat called Chaly which appears on most of their album covers.

E.vil
N.ever
D.ies

Overkill

Opposite, Above: British Metalcore band **Bring Me The Horizon** looked very youthful when formed in 2004 (L–R: Lee Malia, Jordan Fish, Oli Sykes, Matt Nicholls, and Matt Kean).

Opposite, Center: Luke Kilpatrick, Ben Gordon, and Jia O'Connor of Australian Metalcore **Parkway Drive** in May 2011. Formed in 2002, their signature screamed vocals make it hard to discern the lyrics.

Opposite, Below: Singer Martin Engler of the German Gothic Rock band **Mono Inc.** Formed in 2003 they are seen here ten years later in Berlin.

Above: L–R: Tomas Haake of Swedish Metal band **Meshuggah**, German Metal singer-songwriter Doro (Dorothee Pesch) ex-**Warlock**, and Ol Drake of English metal band **Evile** pose for *Metal Hammer*, July 6, 2010.

Right: Formed by guitarist and growl vocalist Mark Jansen after he left **After Forever**, **Epica's** debut album, *The Phantom Agony*, was released in 2003. Combined with the voices of Simone Simons and, since 2009, Isaac Delahaye, Jansen's "unclean" vocals give the Dutch Symphonic Metal band a distinctive sound. A June 2014 photo.

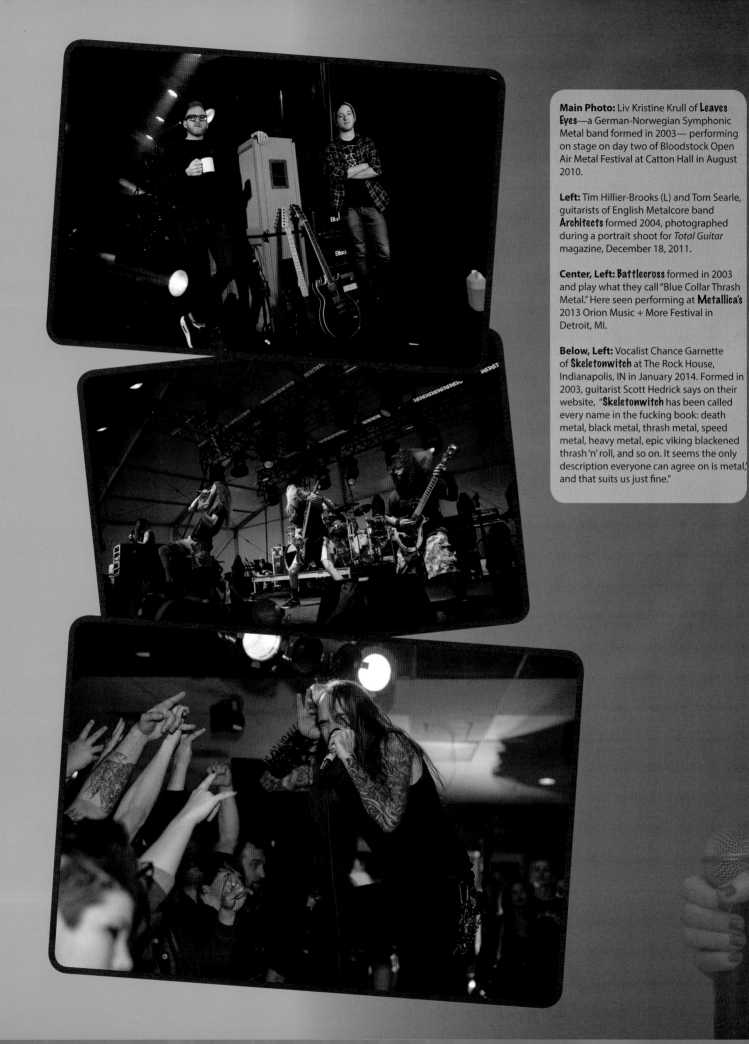

Main Photo: Liv Kristine Krull of **Leaves Eyes**—a German-Norwegian Symphonic Metal band formed in 2003— performing on stage on day two of Bloodstock Open Air Metal Festival at Catton Hall in August 2010.

Left: Tim Hillier-Brooks (L) and Tom Searle, guitarists of English Metalcore band **Architects** formed 2004, photographed during a portrait shoot for *Total Guitar* magazine, December 18, 2011.

Center, Left: Battlecross formed in 2003 and play what they call "Blue Collar Thrash Metal." Here seen performing at **Metallica's** 2013 Orion Music + More Festival in Detroit, MI.

Below, Left: Vocalist Chance Garnette of **Skeletonwitch** at The Rock House, Indianapolis, IN in January 2014. Formed in 2003, guitarist Scott Hedrick says on their website, "**Skeletonwitch** has been called every name in the fucking book: death metal, black metal, thrash metal, speed metal, heavy metal, epic viking blackened thrash 'n' roll, and so on. It seems the only description everyone can agree on is metal," and that suits us just fine."

HEAVY METAL THE STORY IN PICTURES

Above Left: L–R: Ben Carter, Matt Drake, and Joel Graham formed British Thrash Metal band **Evile** in 2004. They have produced four albums to date and are seen performing at Hammerfest in March 2012.

Above: John Kevill (L) and Andy Laux of **Warbringer**. The Thrash Metal exponents formed in high school in 2004 but have undergone many personnel changes since then—most recently seeing the arrival of of Jeff Potts (guitar) and Ben Mottsman (bass), both formerly of **Mantic Ritual**.

Left: Richard "Big Dad Ritch" Anderson and Cord Pool of **Texas Hippie Coalition**. Formed in 2004 Big Dad Ritch describes the band thus on the website: "It's like Lynyrd Skynyrd and ZZ Top had a child, and **Pantera** ended up raising it. We're Red Dirt Metal. That's a flag we wave high. There wasn't a line formed for us, so I created a line and jumped to the front of that bad boy. *Ride On* [their fourth album] is the best example of what we do."

Opposite: **Melissa Auf Der Maur** poses in the media room at the eleventh annual *Kerrang* Awards 2004 in London. Alternative Metal and alt rocker, she is a polymath singer-songwriter, photographer, and occasional actress who is recognized as a major force in modern music.

We're red dirt metal. That's a flag we wave high.

Big Dad Ritch about **Texas Hippie Coalition**

Top: Thomas Vikstrom (R) and Lori Lewis of **Therion** on stage during Bloodstock in August 2011 in the UK. They are a Swedish Symphonic Metal band founded by Christofer Johnsson in 1987.

Above: Six-piece melodic Doom Metal band **Ghost Brigade** comes from Finland and was formed in 2005. Seen here at Party.San Metal Open Air, Germany, in August 2015.

Right: Tim "Ripper" Owens, formerly lead singer of **Judas Priest** but now with **Beyond Fear** and **Rising Force**, performs on stage during Marshall Amp's 50th Anniversary at Wembley Arena in London on September 22, 2012.

Opposite: Chris Cerulli of **Motionless In White** (aka **MIW**) formed 2005, on stage in Manchester, England in September 2013. Their distinctive atmospheric keyboard noises help to give rise to their label of Horror Metal.

Main Photo: Max Cavalera of **Cavalera Conspiracy** in June 2008 at Download Festival. Originally formed as **Inflikted** in 2007 by the reunited Cavalera brothers (both ex **Sepultura**), in 2009 they became **Cavalera Conspiracy** for legal reasons.

Opposite, Above: Spencer Sotelo of Progressive Metal **Periphery** (formed 2005). Considered pioneers of djent music, the band is known for its soaring melodies and poly-rhythmic patterns. Here, live at The Fillmore Charlotte in January, 2015 in Charlotte, NC. "Djent" was inspired and named by Sweden's tech-metal pioneers **Meshuggah**.

Opposite, Center: Phil Bozeman of **Whitechapel**. Formed in 2006 in Knoxville, TX and named after the area of London where Jack the Ripper operated, they play Deathcore Metal. On stage in Cincinnati, OH in July 2012.

Opposite, Below: Daniel O'Sullivan of **Ulver** on stage during Damnation Festival at Leeds University in November 2011. They are a Norwegian experimental musical collective founded in 1993 by vocalist Kristoffer Rygg.

Main Photo: Operatically trained Jill Janus has a vocal range of four octaves and is the lead singer of Doom-influenced Heavy Metal **Huntress**. Formed in 2009 in Los Angeles, they have released three albums and are performing here in January 2014.

Above: Metalcore **Killswitch Engage** formed in 1999 and are shown here in 2003. They use a combination of screaming vocals, growls, and singing to convey their Metalcore style.

Time will always be the thing that kills me truly.

From "Rain" on *Trivium*'s *Ascendancy*
(2005)

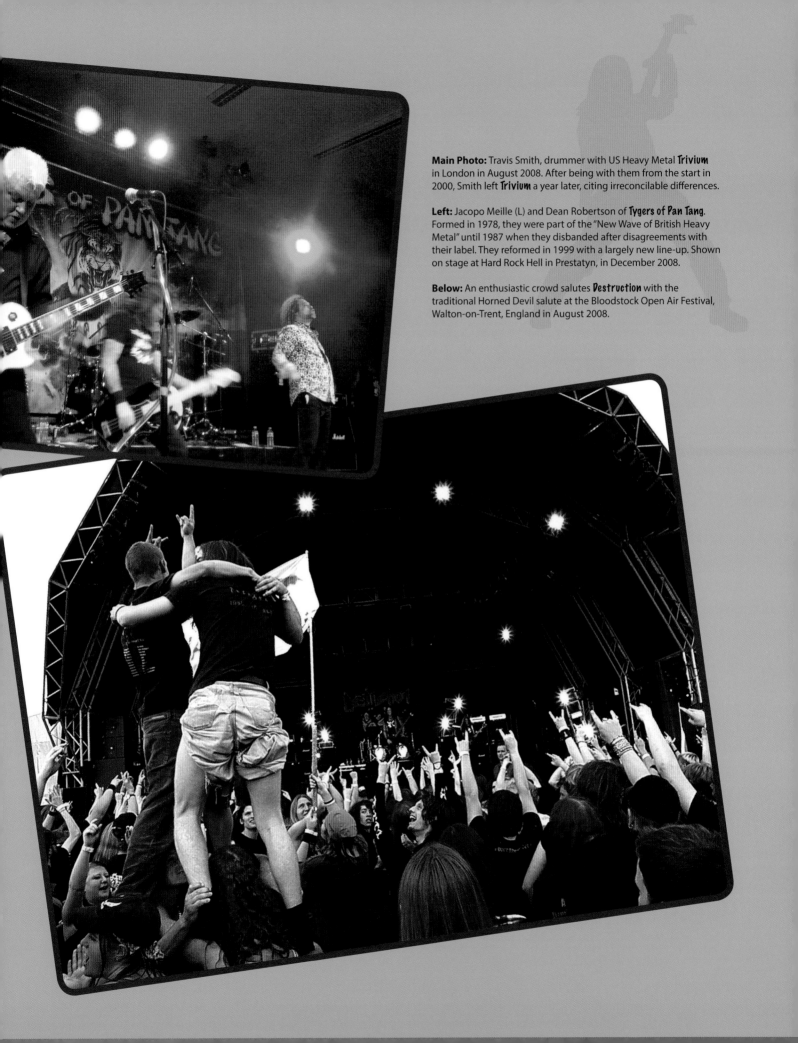

Main Photo: Travis Smith, drummer with US Heavy Metal **Trivium** in London in August 2008. After being with them from the start in 2000, Smith left **Trivium** a year later, citing irreconcilable differences.

Left: Jacopo Meille (L) and Dean Robertson of **Tygers of Pan Tang**. Formed in 1978, they were part of the "New Wave of British Heavy Metal" until 1987 when they disbanded after disagreements with their label. They reformed in 1999 with a largely new line-up. Shown on stage at Hard Rock Hell in Prestatyn, in December 2008.

Below: An enthusiastic crowd salutes **Destruction** with the traditional Horned Devil salute at the Bloodstock Open Air Festival, Walton-on-Trent, England in August 2008.

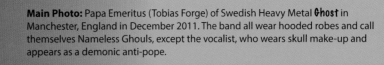

Main Photo: Papa Emeritus (Tobias Forge) of Swedish Heavy Metal **Ghost** in Manchester, England in December 2011. The band all wear hooded robes and call themselves Nameless Ghouls, except the vocalist, who wears skull make-up and appears as a demonic anti-pope.

Below: Influential Swedish epic Doom Metal **Candlemass** was established in Stockholm in 1984 by bassist, songwriter, and bandleader Leif Edling and drummer Matz Ekström. After releasing five full-length albums and touring extensively throughout the 1980s and early 1990s, **Candlemass** disbanded in 1994, but reunited three years later. They broke again in 2002, then reformed in 2004 and have continued to record and perform since then. **Candlemass** is the seventh bestselling Swedish act, having sold over fifteen million albums worldwide.

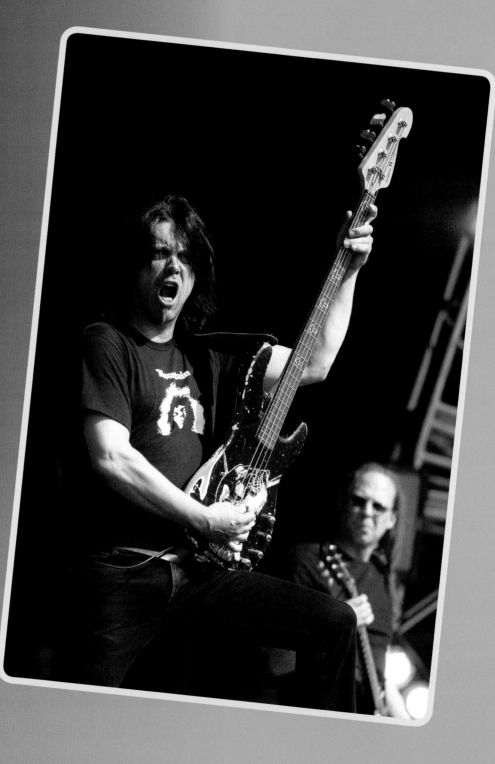

Main Photo: Since their foundation in 1993 in Bakersfield, CA, **Korn** have released forty-one singles of which twenty-eight have charted, plus they have collected numerous industry awards. If nothing else, this all proves that Heavy Metal has a considerable main stream audience.

Opposite: Parody Glam Metal rockers **Steel Panther** formed in Los Angeles in 2000 and are shown here in 2010. They are known for their funny and frequently profane lyrics.

Right: Liquid Tension Experiment are/were a loose group of avant-garde Progressive Metal/Jazz Fusion instrumental musicians who were mostly active in the late 1990s. Seen here at Nearfest in 2008 when they got together again.

Left: Fred Durst of **Limp Bizkit** during MTV Icon Metallica Rehearsal Day2 at Universal Studios, CA, in May 2003. The Rap Metallers formed in 1994 in the underground scene in Florida, went on hiatus 2006–2009 when they started touring again.

Below: Melodic Death Metal **Dethklok** were formed to play the music of virtual band "Dethklok" for the US animated tv series *Metalocalypse* in live shows as here in Atlanta, GA in November 2009.

Opposite: Mortiis started as a solo story-telling project for Norwegian singer Håvard Ellefsen and slowly developed into a band of changing personnel. Ellefsen is the only constant in the line-up.

There's still no party like a Limp Bizkit party.

Rick Florino reviewing a Ft. Lauderdale gig on artistdirect.com

Left: Mikael Stanne and guitarist Niklas Sundin of Swedish Melodic Death Metal **Dark Tranquillity** (formed 1989) on stage at The Bloodstock Open Air Festival, in August 2007. Of the original line up only Sundin and Anders Jivarp remain.

Below: Norwegian Black Metal **Satyricon** at the Double Door in Chicago, IL on October 19, 2009. Founded 1991, their 1996 *Nemesis Divina* is a standout album.

Bottom: **Wolves In The Throne Room** was started in 2003 by the Weaver brothers in Seattle. In 2006, their *Diadem Of 12 Stars* proved a memorable Black Metal moment. Here Nathan Weaver on stage during ATP Festival at Alexandra Palace in May 2012.

Opposite: Drummer and percussionist Dave Witte of crossover Thrash Metal **Municipal Waste** poses to show off his tattoos, in May 2007. He has collaborated and drummed for numerous metal bands and is revered particularly for his rapid playing.

Right: Swedish Progressive Metal **Opeth** at The Forum in London in November 2005. Formed in Stockholm in 1990, they play a mix of jazz, folk, progressive, blues, and classical metal.

Below: Metallica in 2017. Lars Ullrich has been drumming for the band (alongside vocalist and rhythm guitarist James Hetfield) since their foundation in 1981. The other long-serving member, lead guitar Kirk Hammett, joined in 1983.

Opposite: Heavy Metal **Bullet For My Valentine** was formed in 1998 in Wales (shown in 2004). They are influenced by classic Heavy Metal bands and were originally called **Jeff Killed John**.

Opposite: Heavy Metal **Annihilator** were formed in 1984 in Canada. Since then they have enjoyed a measure of success, although numerous musicians have passed through the line-up. Shown in Manchester in 2007.

Left: Mike Clark playing for **Suicidal Tendencies** (founded 1981). Another band that has had numerous changes of personnel, Clark was active 1987–2012.

Below: Ville Valo of Gothic Metal Finnish band **H.I.M.** (short for His Infernal Majesty) and **Mortiis** founder Håvard Ellefsen (aka Mortiis) in 2007. **H.I.M.** folded in 2017 after sales of over ten million records.

Main Photo: Vocalist Bobby "Blitz" Ellsworth fronts Thrash Metal, **Overkill,** he and D.D. Verni are the only regular members to have survived the years. The band formed in 1980 but didn't release an album until 1985. Now, they are one of the oldest Thrash Metal bands still playing and recording.

Above: Doriano Magliano of Metalcore **Woe, Is Me**. Founded in Atlanta, GA in 2009; after numerous changes of line-up the band folded in 2013 (soon after this gig in Cincinnati OH). Only Kevin Hanson lasted from start to finish.

Opposite, Inset: **Trivium**. L–R: Paolo Gregoletto, Matt Heafy, Corey Beaulieu, and Travis Smith in London in August 2008.

Above: Grindcore **Napalm Death**'s Mark "Barney" Greenway (L) and Shane Embury. Coming from the English Midlands they formed in 1981, to date they have released fifteen studio albums. (All the original members had left by late 1986). They are shown here at Bloodstock Open Air Festival in August 2008.

Left: Bjorn Gelotte of Swedish Melodic Death Metal **In Flames**, live on stage at the *Metal Hammer* Golden God Awards, June 2008.

Opposite: Anders Friden of **In Flames**. Founded in 1990 by guitarist Jesper Strömblad as a side project from his then-current Death Metal band, **Ceremonial Oath**, **In Flames** has sold over 2,000,000 records worldwide. Strömblad left the band in February 2010. They are characterized by their growled and screamed vocals over harmonized lead guitar melodies.

There's a reason a band like this elicits such passion from fans.

Adrien Begrand about **In Flames**
on popmatters.com

Left: Will Palmer of **Angel Witch** at Hard Rock Hell in 2009, Wales. They formed in London in 1977 since when they have had numerous changes of line-up. They play to critical acclaim but disappointing popular support.

Opposite, Above: L–R: Glenn Five, Robb Reiner, and Steve "Lips" Kudlow of **Anvil** at Giants Stadium in July 2009. Reiner and Kudlow are original members from foundation in 1978.

Opposite, Below: Johan Soderberg of Swedish Melodic Death Metal **Amon Amarth** (founded 1992). Sometimes dubbed Viking Metal, they sing of Swedish history, mythology, and particularly, Vikings. At Download Festival in June 2008.

Just a power- house in the world of Death Metal.

Sol about **Amon Amarth's** Jomsviking on metalinjection.net

Opposite: Amon Amarth (the local name of J.R.R. Tolkien's Mount Doom) on a real Viking longboat on the River Thames in Richmond, in September 2009.

Above: Anders Nystrom and Mattias Norrman of Katatonia on the first day of Bloodstock festival in August 2009.

Right: Vocalist and bassist Tom Angelripper of Sodom. Founded in 1981, they are regarded as one of "The Big Teutonic Four" of German Thrash Metal. Seen at Bloodstock in August 2009.

Main Photo: Jeff Walker of English Death Metal **Carcass** on the first day of Bloodstock in August 2009. Their gruesome lyrics and stage performance made them pioneers of Grindcore when they founded in 1985.

Right: Trey Williams of US Technical Death Metal **Dying Fetus** on stage in Sheffield, England in October 2009. The band formed in 1991 with Williams joining in 2007.

Opposite, Above: V Santura joined as touring guitarist for Swiss Extreme Metal **Celtic Frost** in 2008, just before the band folded due to irreconcilable differences.

Opposite, Below: Franco Sesa drummed and played percussion with **Celtic Frost** between 2002–2008.

Below: Al Jourgesen of **Ministry**, one of the pioneering Industrial Metal bands (founded 1981) from the United States. Playing at the Kentish Town Forum in August 2006 with the then new line up including Paul Raven ex-**Killing Joke** on bass and Joey Jordison ex-**Slipknot** on drums. After a three-year hiatus (2008–2011), **Ministry** reformed and have produced three studio albums.

Right: Swedish guitarist Michael Amott of Death Metal **Arch Enemy** and seminal Grindcore **Carcass** in November 2007.

Opposite, Top: Melodic Death Metal **Arch Enemy** comes from Sweden. On formation in 1995, the band members were all veterans of other metal bands. Seen here in 2014 with Alissa White-Gluz as lead vocal.

Opposite, Below: Lenzig Leal of Colorado Grindcore **Cephalic Carnage** and Nick Schendzielos on bass in 2007. They call their style "rocky mountain hydro grind."

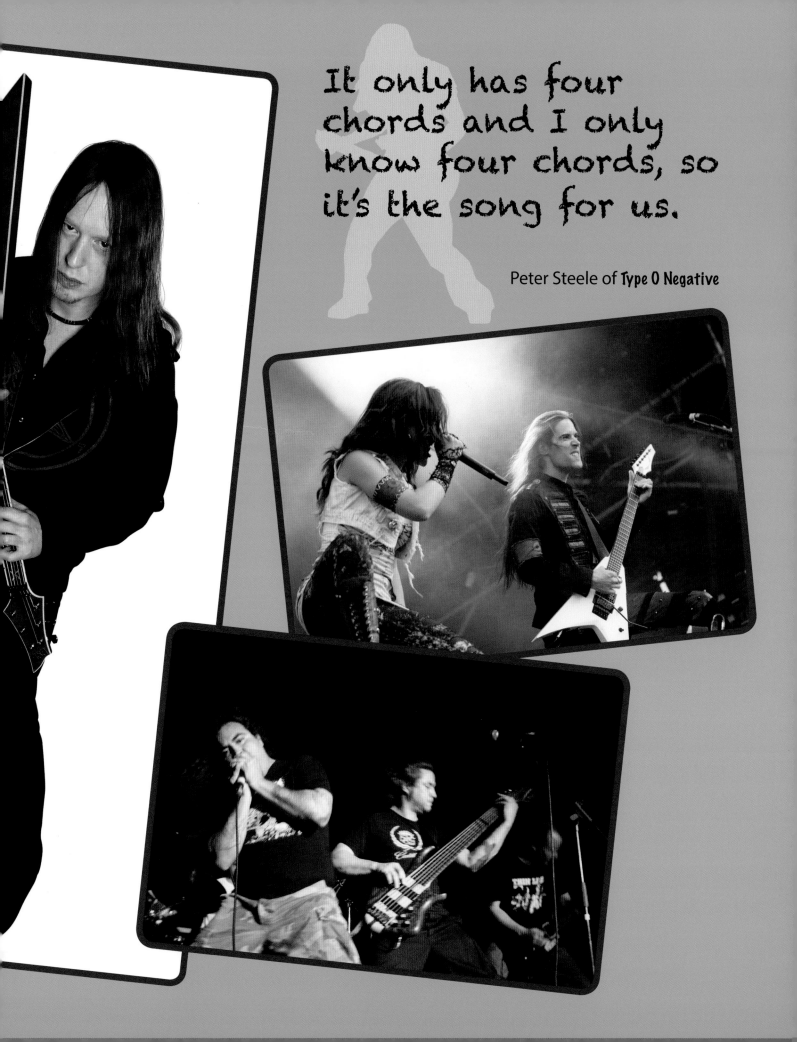

It only has four chords and I only know four chords, so it's the song for us.

Peter Steele of **Type O Negative**

Top: Tomas "OBeast" Koefoed of **Mnemic** played bass with the band 2003 to 2011. The band formed 1998 in Denmark and played what they described as Future Fusion Metal—literally a mixture of various Metal genres. After five albums they have been on hiatus since 2013.

Above: Markus Grosskopf (L) and Andi Deris of **Helloween** in 2008. Formed in 1984, the German Power Metal band has produced fourteen studio albums, although the lineup today is very different from when it started. Markus Grosskopf is (with Michael Weikath) a founder member, Andi Deris joined in 1994.

Left: US Post Hardcore Punk **Converge** formed 1990. Jacob Bannon (visuals, vocals, and lyrics), seen at the Hove Festival in June 2008. They are considered to be one of the most original bands to emerge from the American punk underground.

Below: Adam Dutkiewicz, of **Killswitch Engage** at Rawk Attack, Hamburg, Germany in 2016. They were one of the early pioneers of Metalcore and are proven festival favorites.

6. METAL TODAY

In the ever-expanding universe that is metal music, new combinations and connections are constantly being forged. In the second decade of this century, the definition of a "metal band" has been stretched far beyond what anyone might have imagined forty years ago.

Take San Francisco's **Deafheaven**, for example. They combine some of the elements of Black Metal with a dense haze of guitar distortion, a sound that verges on what is often called "shoegaze." The effect is dizzying.

Or take **Blut Aus Nord** from Normandy, France. Their *777* album trilogy blended Black Metal with almost danceable beats and a healthy helping of industrial noise. They make a sound that is at once familiar and very new.

Kvelertak are from Norway and their name is Norwegian for "stranglehold." Their three-guitar lineup makes music that is recognizably Norwegian metal but otherwise defies description, lurching between many styles, often within the same song. The effect is nothing short of dazzling.

Pallbearer—from Little Rock, AR, are ostensibly a Doom Metal band but in fact are so much more. Their sound has some of the widescreen drama of the **Blue Öyster Cult** and the intricacy of progressive rock.

Californian singer/songwriter Chelsea Wolfe blends elements of folk and metal with industrial and electronic grooves. Her albums *Abyss* and *Hiss Spun* garnered critical raves.

Pittsburgh's **Code Orange** are a Hardcore Punk outfit who manage to completely transcend the genre with the deceptive complexity of their music. Their 2017 album *Forever* was top of many "Best Of" lists.

Arcane Roots are a former Hardcore band from Kingston Upon Thames, England. They completely reinvented their sound for second album *Melancholia Hymns* to include electronic percussion and textures.

One current trend that can't be ignored is the onomatopoeically named "djent" style of guitar playing pioneered by Swedish band **Meshuggah** and expanded by the likes of **SiKth** from Watford, England. The djent player will employ dense layers of polyphonic arpeggiating combined with syncopated palm muting and riffing.

Many of the players mentioned above were barely born during the Grunge era, never mind the Thrash era that preceded it, or the other stages of heavy music that stretch back fifty years or more. Every year a new crop of youngsters take up axes and drums to forge their own unique form of the music, and as a result, Heavy Metal is a music that will never stop reinventing itself.

Fred Durst of **Limp Bizkit** on stage during the last date of the Kerrang Tour at Brixton Academy on February 21, 2014.

T1MELINE

2010

March
Option Paralysis is fourth album from **The Dillinger Escape Plan**

April
Glam rockers **Ratt** are back with *Infestation*

May
Sacramento Alternative Metal band **Deftones** release sixth album *Diamond Eyes*

Ronnie James Dio dies of stomach cancer

June
Norway's **Kvelertak** release stylistically diverse eponymous debut

Ozzy Osbourne is back with *Scream*

July
Buckinghamshire, UK band **Young Guns** release debut *All Our Kings Are Dead*

August
Iron Maiden do it again with fifteenth album *The Final Frontier*

September
Swedish Symphonic Black Metal band **Dimmu Borgir** release their ninth album, *Abrahadabra*

October
Jerusalem Black Metal band **Melechesh** release fifth album *The Epigenesis*

January
New Zealand Technical Death Metal band **Ulcerate** issue third album *The Destroyers of All*

June
Brooklyn Post Metal band **Tombs** release second album *Path of Totality*

August
Trivium push boundaries with fifth album *In Waves*

September
Unto the Locust is acclaimed seventh album from **Machine Head**

Mastodon are back with *The Hunter*

October
Lou Reed and **Metallica** make album *Lulu* based

on plays by Frank Wedekind

November
Megadeth are back with *Th1rt3en*

From Calvados, France, avant-garde Groove Metal band **Blut Aus Nord** release their ninth album, *777-The Desanctification*

March
Meshuggah release seventh album *Koloss*

May
Fourth album from **The Dillinger Escape Plan** is *One of Us Is the Killer*

June
Fifth album from **Linkin Park** is *Living Things*

July
Testament unleash thier tenth album *Dark Roots of the Earth*

Sludge Metal band **Baroness** from Savannah, Georgia, release third album *Yellow & Green*

October
Neurosis release their tenth album *Honor Found In Decay*

Virginia Grindcore band **Pig Destroyer** release fifth album *Book Burner*

November
Deftones release highly regarded seventh album *Koi No Yokan*

January
Straight Out of Hell is fourteenth album for Germany's **Helloween**

April
Swedish Doom Metal band **Ghost** release second album *Infestissumam*

Deep Purple release nineteenth album *Now What?!*

June
San Francisco's **Deafheaven** combine emo and shoegaze with Death Metal on second album *Sunbather*, and are loved by critics

Ozzy returns to **Black Sabbath** with *13*

2011
2012
2013

August
Colored Sands is first album in twelve years from Canada's **Gorguts**

October
San Diego-based **Earthless** bring some vintage instrumental hard rock with third album *From the Ages*

Motörhead are back with *Aftershock*

February
Behemoth release tenth album *The Satanist*

March
Eleventh album from **Gamma Ray** is *Empire of the Undead*

April
Triptykon (featuring former **Celtic Frost** front man Thomas Gabriel Fischer) releases second album *Melana Chasmata*

May
Folk Metal band **Agalloch** release fifth and final album *The Serpent & the Sphere*

Eyehategod (EHG) release their self-titled fifth album, but lose drummer Joe LaCaze during the process

August
Opeth return with *Pale Communion*

September
Doom Metal band **YOB** from Oregon release seventh album *Clearing the Path to Ascend*

October
Soused is a collaboration between Scott Walker and **Sunn O)))**

Fifth album from **At the Gates** is *At War with Reality*

Cream bassist and singer Jack Bruce dies at 71

January
Marylin Manson comes back with ninth album *The Pale Emperor*

Maryland's **Turnstiles** release debut album *Nonstop Feeling*

April
Cello metal is back with *Shadowmaker*, eighth album from **Apocalyptica**

May
Faith No More return from hiatus with critically acclaimed album *Sol Invictus*

June
High on Fire release seventh album *Luminiferous*

July
Cradle of Filth's *Hammer of the Witches*

August
San Diego's **Cattle Decapitation** turn in seventh album *The Anthropocene Extinction*

September
Iron Maiden show the youngsters how it's done with *The Book of Souls*

December
Motörhead's Lemmy dies, age 70

January
Megadeth return with *Dystopia*

April
Deftones issue eighth album *Gore*

May
Kvelertak release third album *Nattesferd*

June
Magma is French Prog Metal **Gojira's** sixth album

September
Eleventh album from **Neurosis** is *Fires Within Fires*

October
Debut album *Gold,* from **Sludge Metal Whores**

November
Metallica get back to their roots with *Hardwired... to Self Destruct*

January
Sepultura return with *Machine Messiah*

March
Ice T's **Body Count** issues sixth album *Bloodlust*

May
Soundgarden's Chris Cornell commits suicide

June
UK djent pioneers **SiKth** release fourth album *The Future In Whose Eyes?*

July
Linkin Park's Chester Bennington commits suicide

August
Queens of the Stone Age release *Villains*

November
Wizard Bloody Wizard is ninth album from Dorset Doom Metal band **Electric Wizard**

Metalcore veterans **Converge** release ninth album *The Dusk In Us*

December
Morbid Angel return with *Kingdoms Disdained*

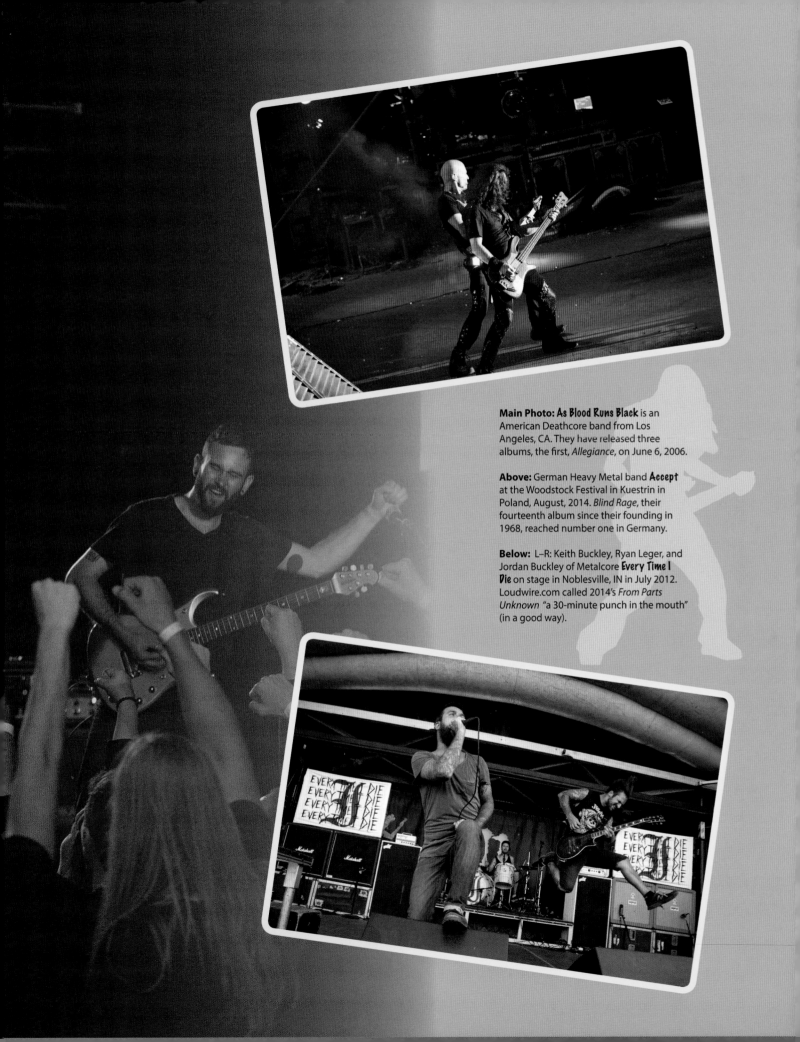

Main Photo: As Blood Runs Black is an American Deathcore band from Los Angeles, CA. They have released three albums, the first, *Allegiance*, on June 6, 2006.

Above: German Heavy Metal band **Accept** at the Woodstock Festival in Kuestrin in Poland, August, 2014. *Blind Rage*, their fourteenth album since their founding in 1968, reached number one in Germany.

Below: L–R: Keith Buckley, Ryan Leger, and Jordan Buckley of Metalcore **Every Time I Die** on stage in Noblesville, IN in July 2012. Loudwire.com called 2014's *From Parts Unknown* "a 30-minute punch in the mouth" (in a good way).

To me it all
comes across
as being
comical, as
being a
parody of
itself.

Trent Reznor of
Nine Inch Nails

Opposite: Vocalist Shagrath, of Norwegian Symphonic Metal band **Dimmu Borgir**, on stage during day three of Bloodstock in August 2012 in Derby, United Kingdom.

Above Right: American Nu Metal band **Korn** lead guitarists James "Munky" Shaffer and Brian "Head" Welsh pose for a September 1998 portrait with their seven-string guitars. 1998 was the year Nu Metal broke into the mainstream, with Korn's third album, *Follow the Leader*, which peaked at number one on the *Billboard 200*.

Right: Cristina Scabbia of **Lacuna Coil** performs at The Roundhouse in November 2013 in London, England.

Above: August 16, 2014, Tokyo: members of Japan's pop group **Babymetal**, L–R: Moameta, Su-Metal, and Yuimetal. They were founded in 2010 as a "fusion of metal and (Japanese) idol" music. When playing live they are backed by the Kami Band who are members of various Japanese metal bands.

Right: Norwegian band **Kvelertak** formed in Stavanger in 2007. Their name translates as stranglehold and their music certainly grabs you by the throat. They opened for **Metallica** on the European leg of their WorldWired Tour between September 2017 and May 2018.

Below: Founders of **Butcher Babies** Carla Harvey (center) and Heidi Shepherd with Henry Flury. In performance at the H&H MetalFest 2014.

Main Photo: Russell Allen (ex **Symphony X**) now of **Adrenaline Mob** at Hard Rock Live! in April 2014 in Hollywood, FL. They formed in 2011 and within six months were playing live.

Above: L–R: Erik Tisinger, Chase Brickenden, Mario Rubio, and Evan Seidlitz of Thrash Metal **Thrown Into Exile** in October 2013 in Pomona, CA. They formed in 2011 and made their reputation touring extensively around the US.

Below: L–R: Will Hunt (ex **Evanescence**), David Draiman (ex **Disturbed**), and Geno Lenardo (ex **Filter**) formed Industrial Metal band **Device**. Seen here in 2013 backstage in Columbus, OH.

Main Photo: Finnish Melodic Folk Metal **Ensiferum** have had many changes of line-up: here they are performing at Rockharz Open Air, in Ballenstedt Germany in 2018. The band has released seven studio albums, the last *Two Paths* in 2017 featuring accordionist Netta Skog, who left two months after the album was released.

Opposite: Jari Mäenpää of **Wintersun** (formerly of **Ensiferum**) on stage during Bloodstock Open Air Festival in August 2011 in Derby, England. They use harsh and clean vocals over fast music and creative folk harmonies.

Main Photo: L–R: Tomasz "Orion" Wróblewski, Adam "Nergal" Darski and Patryk "Seth" Sztyber of Polish Blackened Death Metal **Behemoth**, live on stage at Sonisphere festival, Warsaw, in June 2010. They formed in 1991 in the Gdansk metal underground scene and then developed their own unique style.

Opposite: Foxy of **SSS** (aka **Short, Sharp, Shock**) on stage during Damnation Festival at Leeds University in November 2010, England. They are a Crossover Thrash band formed in Liverpool, England in 2010.

Opposite: Megadeth at the Summer Breeze Open Air in 2017. One of the "Big Four" of American Thrash Metal, the band have been playing since 1983 during which time they have shifted over thirty-eight milliion records worldwide.

Opposite, Inset: Vocalist Erik Danielsson of **Watain** on stage in London in December 2013. Watain formed in 1998 and describe themselves as "theistic Satanists." They are a Swedish Black Metal band from Uppsala and have released five albums since 2000 including *The Wild Hunt*, which went to number one in Sweden.

Left: Michael Poulsen of Danish Heavy Metal **Volbeat** at the Louder Than Life Festival in Louisville, KT, in 2014. They have achieved international success and are massively popular back home in Denmark.

Below: Kvelertak lead singer Erlend Hjelvik wears his famous owl outfit on stage during the band's gig at Amager Bio in Copenhagen, Denmark, in 2013. The owl has become Kvelertak's mascot since their bass player Marvin Nygaard suggested using it in about 2006 for some homemade CD covers for friends.

Main Photo: Stian Thoresen of **Dimmu Borgir** on stage during Sziget Festival in August 2012 in Budapest, Hungary. Only Shagrath (Stian Tomt Thoresen) and Silenoz (Sven Atle Kopperud) are original members from its foundation in 1993.

Right: Power and Speed Metal **Gamma Ray's** at the Rockharz Open Air, Ballenstedt, Germany in 2016. They are one of the biggest German Heavy Metal bands.

Below: Bassist and vocalist Ian Kilmister, better known by his stage name Lemmy, of British hard rock group **Motörhead** live on stage at the 2013 Golden Gods Awards in the O2 Arena, London, in June 2013. He died two years later, at the age of 70, unrepentant and living hard to the last!

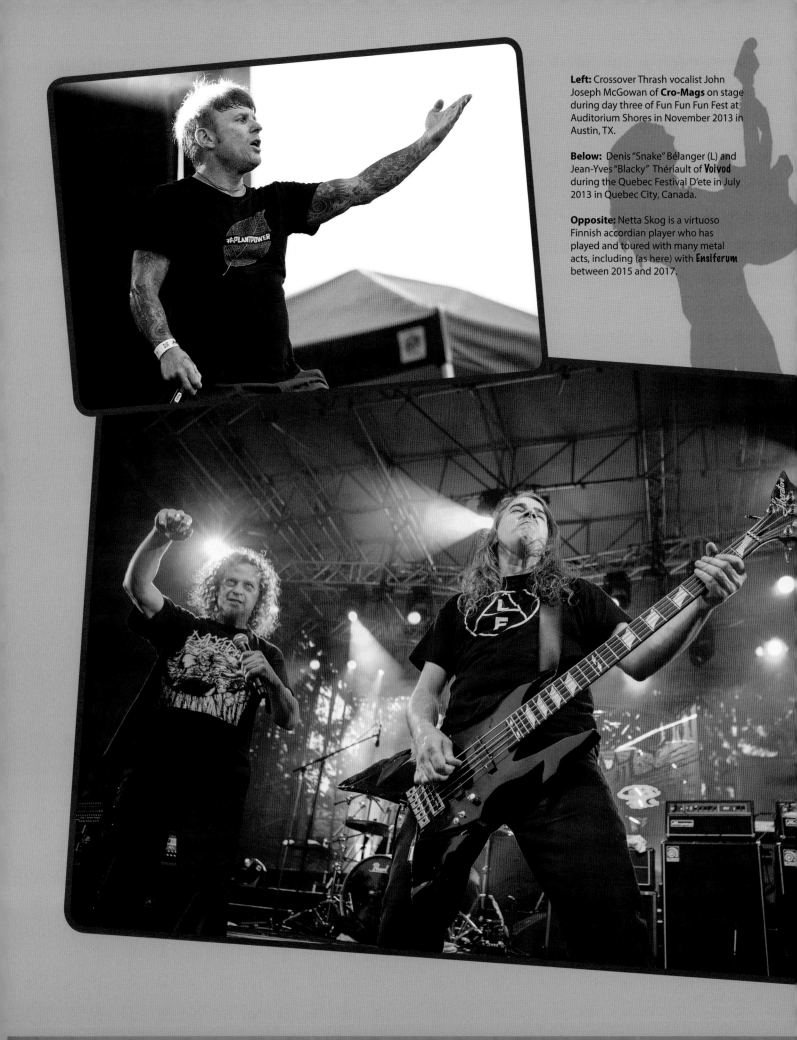

Left: Crossover Thrash vocalist John Joseph McGowan of **Cro-Mags** on stage during day three of Fun Fun Fun Fest at Auditorium Shores in November 2013 in Austin, TX.

Below: Denis "Snake" Bélanger (L) and Jean-Yves "Blacky" Thériault of **Voivod** during the Quebec Festival D'ete in July 2013 in Quebec City, Canada.

Opposite: Netta Skog is a virtuoso Finnish accordian player who has played and toured with many metal acts, including (as here) with **Ensiferum** between 2015 and 2017.

Main Photo: Lead vocalist Danny Worsnop of Metalcore **Asking Alexandria** on stage in December 2013 in London. The band formed in north Yorkshire in 2008 and in January 2015, Worsnop announced his departure to concentrate on his new band **We Are Harlot**.

Right: Kirk Hammett of **Metallica** (L) playing with Thrash Metal **Death Angel** at Kirk Von Hammett's Fear FestEvil in February 2014 in San Francisco, CA.

Below: Vocalist Rafal "Rasta" Piotrowski of Polish Technical Death Metal **Decapitated** in November 2014 in Seattle, WA. The band originally formed in 1996, folded in 2007, then reformed in 2009 when Piotrowski joined the band.

Main Photo: Doom Metal **Hamferð** come from the Faroe Islands. They take their inspiration from their remote homeland, "where the sea and the long cold winter play the major role as main contributors." Seen here at Underground in Wuppertal, November 2014.

Below: Gene Hoglan of **Testament.** Currently a five-piece Thrash Metal band, only founder member Eric Peterson still remains. Since their foundation in 1983, fifteen other band members have come and gone.

Opposite, Below: Thrash Metal **Exodus** formed in California in 1980 and have had a chequered career with numerous line-ups. Shown here is bassist Jack Gibson (joined 1997) in November 2014 in Oakland, CA. They welcomed back vocalist Steve "Zetro" Souza for *Blood In, Blood Out* their tenth studio album in 2014.

Opposite, Above: Singer Chester Bennington and Dave Farrell of **Linkin Park** during the MTVu Fandom Awards at Comic-Con International 2014 at PETCO Park in July 2014 in San Diego, CA.

Opposite, Below: Bassist Troy Sanders of **Mastodon** in November 2014 in Nashville, TN. They play in a wide variety of metal styles and are considered among the leaders of the New Wave American Heavy Metal that emerged in the mid-1990s.

Above, Left: Brad Delson, Joe Hahn, Mike Shinoda, Chester Bennington, Rob Bourdon, and Dave Farrell of **Linkin Park** in August 2014 in West Palm Beach, FL. *Kerrang!* called them "The Biggest Rock Band in the World Right Now" in 2014.

Below, Left: Formed in 2004 and still with the same line-up, **Alter Bridge** play post grunge-influenced Heavy Metal. Here, guitarist Mark Tremonti during 2014 Rock On The Range in May 2014 in Columbus, OH.

Main Photo: Giulio Moschini, lead guitar of Italian Death Metal **Hour Of Penance**, in March 2013 in Manchester, England.

Above: Best of the Stoner Rock/ Doom Metal sect, Londoners **Orange Goblin** was originally formed in 1995 as **Our Haunted Kingdom**. Vocalist Ben Ward on stage at Download Festival in June 2014.

Right: Synyster Gates from **Avenged Sevenfold** in May 2014 in Columbus, OH. Their album, *Hail to the King* (2013) hit number one in album charts on both sides of the Atlantic.

Opposite: Lead guitar Galder (Tom Rune Andersen)—joined 2000—of **Dimmu Borgir** on stage at Bloodstock in August 2014 in Derby, England.

Right: Drummer Jeremy Spencer of **Five Finger Death Punch** on stage during the October 2014 Louder Than Life Festival in Louisville, KY.

Below: Frontman Beau Bokan (joined in 2008) and guitarist Eric Lambert (joined in 2005) of US Metalcore **Blessthefall** at Download in June 2014. The band itself was founded in Phoenix, AZ, in 2003 by a group of high school friends.

7 METAL GENRES

As the years of the 1980s inevitably progressed into the 1990s, metal splintered into a dizzying array of genres. This began with the synthesis of Metal and Punk pioneered by the New Wave of British Heavy Metal, a movement that included bands such as **Motörhead** (started by ex **Hawkwind** bassist Lemmy), **Iron Maiden**, **Def Leppard**, and **Saxon**. Tempos were faster and riffs more prominent, drawing on some of the more popular early metal songs like **Black Sabbath's** "Paranoid" or **Deep Purple's** "Speed King." Meanwhile in the USA, **Black Flag's** Hardcore Punk style had its own massive influence.

From the outset, as bands in Europe and the USA began to adopt this modern metal style, there was a divergence in approach. Speed Metal adhered to a highly technical level of playing, while Thrash Metal was more inclusive and punk-influenced. European and Scandanavian bands developed their own Black Metal and Death Metal scenes. MTV-friendly Glam Metal (or "Hair Metal") dominated the TV screens. Grunge and Stoner Rock exploded as a reaction against Glam Metal. Gradually, unusual and even unheard-of influences were allowed, leading to such genres as Industrial Metal, Avant-Garde Metal, and Rap Metal. Nu Metal took these styles to platinum sales levels, but was relatively short lived. Groove Metal proved that "dance" tempos and strong melody are always popular, no matter what the musical context.

Meanwhile, the more traditional approach was just as prevalent. Power Metal and Progressive Metal bands would continue to use some of the trademark features of their 1970s forbears. Neoclassical Metal and Symphonic Metal bands took instrumental and vocal prowess to a whole new level.

This chapter will attempt to cover the most prominent of the genres existing today. Some of them, like Rap Metal or Funk Metal, have somewhat petered out … or maybe are just ripe for a revival. Most of them seem to be going from strength to strength. Many of these genres have their own subgenres: within Neoclassical Metal there is Cello Metal, for instance. Or within Symphonic Metal there is Symphonic Goth Metal, Symphonic Doom Metal, and so on.

One thing is for sure. Metal music will continue to evolve and bring on new adherents. New generations will discover the primal thrill of the electric guitar riff and will reinvent it in their own style. And as long as there are fans of exciting and visceral music, metal will live forever.

There are basically two categories of music: Metal and bullshit.

Bruce Dickinson of
Iron Maiden

Mike Mushok of Alternative Metal band **Staind** during 2014 Rock On The Range in May 2014 in Columbus, OH.

ALTERNATIVE METAL

Alternative Metal is the rather all-encompassing term given to a genre of metal that includes elements of Indie and Alternative Rock. Late 1970s UK band **Killing Joke** is often cited as a major early influence. In the mid-1980s, San Francisco band **Faith No More**, who started out at the beginning of the decade as a post-punk band,
began to blend metal styles with funk and indie elements. Another band developing in a similar way was **Jane's Addiction**, whose lead singer Perry Farrell instituted the Lollapallooza festival in 1991. This yearly event was to help break many Alternative Metal acts, including **Tool** and **System Of A Down**.

Based in Los Angeles, **Tool** formed in 1990 and by the middle of the decade albums such as the triple-platinum *Aenima* propelled them to the forefront of the Alternative Metal movement.

System Of A Down also from Southern California, played a kind of pop-honed version of metal that builds on the advances of **Faith No More** and **Jane's Addiction**. They also had multi-platinum success with their album *Toxicity*.

With such disparate bands being included in the same classification, it's little wonder that the Alternative Metal category fractured into many other categories as the 1990s progressed.

Opposite: Daron Malakian, Serj Tankian, Shavo Odadjian, and John Dolmayan of **System of a Down** (aka **SOAD**) at the 25th Annual KROQ Almost Acoustic Christmas at The Forum on December 13, 2014 in Inglewood, CA.

Above: Vocalist Maynard James Keenan of the Alt Metal band **Tool** playing the mainstage at Edge Fest as part of the Canada Day celebrations at Molson Park in Barrie Ontario in July 2001.

Right: Tool live at the Olympia In Paris, France in May 2002. They formed in LA in 1990 and play a mix of progressive, alternative, and art rock.

AVANT-GARDE METAL

This interesting subgenre blends metal with elements of avant-garde music: instruments that have been "treated" or retuned, unusual key signatures and song structures, unusual vocal and electronic textures. The genre is also often referred to as Experimental Metal.

It has roots in the progressive rock pioneered by **King Crimson** and others in the late 1960s and early 1970s. The net of influences is thrown much wider though to include the experimental electronic music of Stockhausen and the dark noise rock of **The Velvet Underground**.

Current prominent bands of the genre include **Boris** from Japan and **Sunn O)))** from Seattle.

Formed in 1992, the prolific **Boris** have released twenty-four studio albums (at the time of writing) as well as numerous singles, EPs and collaborations with other bands. Their album *Pink* was hailed as one of the best of 2006 by *Spin* magazine and others.

Named after their favorite amplifier, **Sunn O)))** have a deep, droning, almost completely non-rhythmic sound. Since their 1999 formation the band have released many albums and collaborations, including *Soused* with the legendary Scott Walker.

Main Photo: Greg Anderson of **Sunn O)))** on stage at HMV Ritz in June 2012 in Manchester, England. They formed in Seattle in 1998 and play Drone Metal extremely loudly.

Inset: Michio Kurihara of **Boris** performs with members of **Sunn O)))** as the band **Altar** at All Tomorrow's Parties, in September 2010 in Monticello, NY.

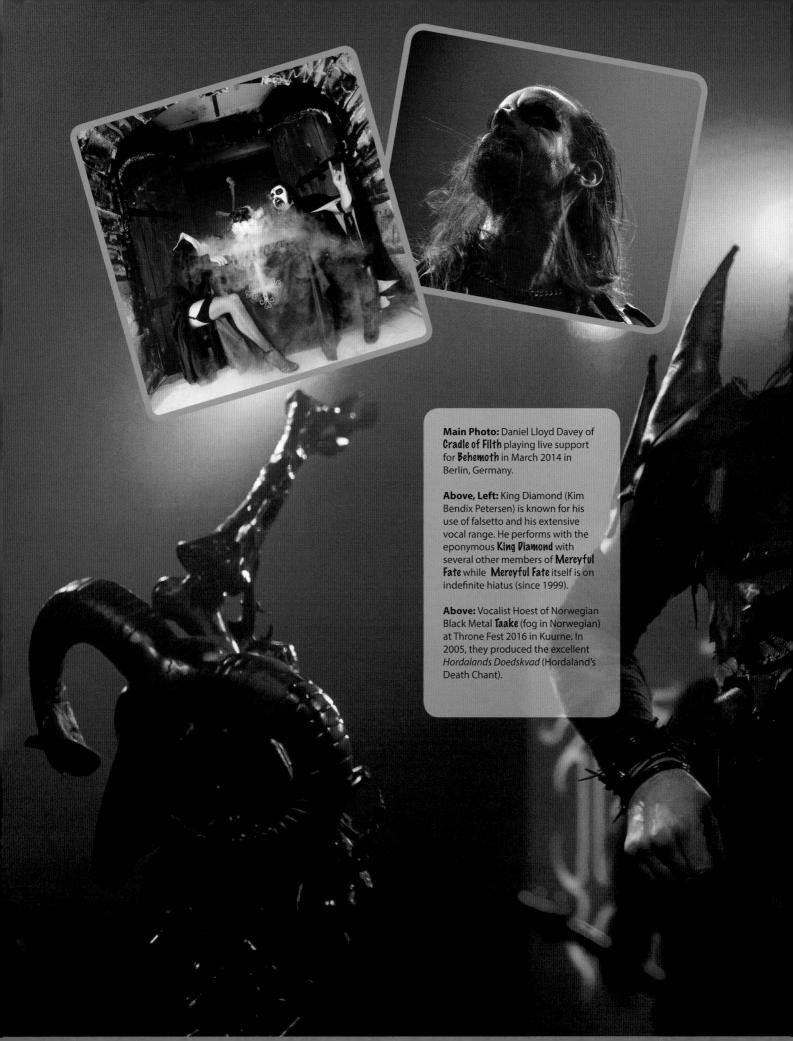

Main Photo: Daniel Lloyd Davey of **Cradle of Filth** playing live support for **Behemoth** in March 2014 in Berlin, Germany.

Above, Left: King Diamond (Kim Bendix Petersen) is known for his use of falsetto and his extensive vocal range. He performs with the eponymous **King Diamond** with several other members of **Mercyful Fate** while **Mercyful Fate** itself is on indefinite hiatus (since 1999).

Above: Vocalist Hoest of Norwegian Black Metal **Taake** (fog in Norwegian) at Throne Fest 2016 in Kuurne. In 2005, they produced the excellent *Hordalands Doedskvad* (Hordaland's Death Chant).

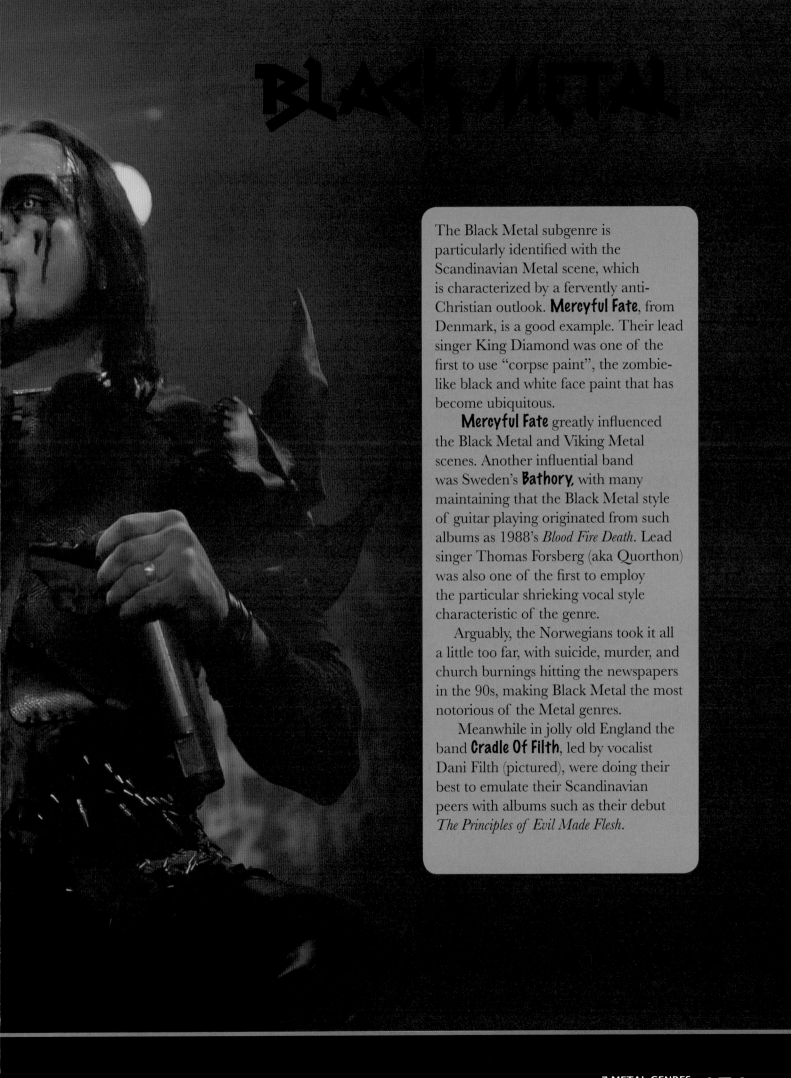

BLACK METAL

The Black Metal subgenre is particularly identified with the Scandinavian Metal scene, which is characterized by a fervently anti-Christian outlook. **Mercyful Fate**, from Denmark, is a good example. Their lead singer King Diamond was one of the first to use "corpse paint", the zombie-like black and white face paint that has become ubiquitous.

Mercyful Fate greatly influenced the Black Metal and Viking Metal scenes. Another influential band was Sweden's **Bathory**, with many maintaining that the Black Metal style of guitar playing originated from such albums as 1988's *Blood Fire Death*. Lead singer Thomas Forsberg (aka Quorthon) was also one of the first to employ the particular shrieking vocal style characteristic of the genre.

Arguably, the Norwegians took it all a little too far, with suicide, murder, and church burnings hitting the newspapers in the 90s, making Black Metal the most notorious of the Metal genres.

Meanwhile in jolly old England the band **Cradle Of Filth**, led by vocalist Dani Filth (pictured), were doing their best to emulate their Scandinavian peers with albums such as their debut *The Principles of Evil Made Flesh*.

CHRISTIAN METAL

Christian Metal is not so much a musical style as an ideological counter to the "negative" and often outright anti-Christian sentiments of mainstream metal music, and has often been called "White Metal" or even "Unblack Metal" to emphasize its opposition to the dark force of Black Metal. Christian Metal bands exist within most of the musical subgenres of metal.

In the 1980s, the Christian Glam Metal band **Stryper** from Southern California became popular enough for even non-Christian fans to attend their gigs, during which Bibles were thrown into the audience. **Stryper** were the first Christian Metal band to achieve platinum status with their album *To Hell With The Devil*. However, their greater exposure also brought its share of hostile receptions, particularly when playing in Europe.

More recently, Florida band **The Almost**, fronted by Aaron Gillespie, have had a lot of success with their melodic post-grunge music, beginning with their debut *Southern Weather*.

Other examples of Christian Metal bands working in different subgenres: **Underoath** (Metalcore), **Tourniquet** (Thrash Metal), **Mortification** (Death Metal), and Sweden's **Narnia** (Progressive Metal).

It's also worth mentioning that some mainstream metal acts have Christian members, including **Linkin Park**, **Iron Maiden**, and **Megadeth**.

Main Photo: Michaell Sweet lead vocals and guitar of Glam Metal **Stryper** at the BamaJam Music and Arts Festival in Alabama in June 2012.

Above: Aaron Gillespie (ex **Underoath**) is founder, drummer, guitarist, and clean vocalist of **The Almost**. The band is on hiatus while Gillespie works as **Paramore's** touring drummer.

DEATH METAL

This genre combines detuned guitars, deep growling vocals and aggressive drumming. Double-kick drum pedals are often employed to maximize the aural assault.

Lyric themes will encompass every dark subject imaginable, from Satanism to torture and murder.

Scream Bloody Gore was the 1987 debut album from Florida band **Death**, and is considered by many to be the first true Death Metal album. They remained very influential and went from strength to strength until founder Chuck Shuldiner died in 2001 from pneumonia.

Swedish band **Avatar** formed in 1991 and at first specialized in melodic Death Metal, which included some elements of 1970s metal. Over the years they have progressed in a more Avant-Metal direction.

Behemoth (from Poland incorporated many different styles into their brand of Death Metal, including Middle Eastern female voices, acoustic guitars and electronic instruments.

Sweden's **Soilwork** is another Death Metal band that employs synthesizers in their music. Formed in 1991, the band has released eleven albums to date.

Florida band **Trivium** formed in 1999 and released its debut album *Ember To Inferno* in 2002. In 2008, their fourth album *Shogun* made number one in the UK Rock Album Chart.

Above, Left: Frontman Bjorn "Speed" Strid of Swedish Melodic Death Metal **Soilwork** at Bloodstock in August 2008. He is the only member of the original band founded in 1995 in Helsingborg, Sweden.

Above: Johannes Eckerström (with John Alfredsson) is one of the original founders of Swedish Death Metal **Avatar**. Shown here during Rock On The Range in May 2014, Columbus, OH.

Opposite, Above: L-R: Nick Augusto and Matt Heafy of **Trivium** in January 2012 in Royal Oak, MI.

Opposite, Below: Patryk "Seth" Sztyber of **Behemoth** at Copenhell, Copenhagen in June 2014. Formerly with **Nomad**, he joined **Behemoth** in 2004 where he plays lead and rhythm guitars and contributes backing vocals.

DOOM METAL

Doom Metal shares the detuned guitars, growling vocals, and percussive assault of Death Metal, but it slows the tempo way down. Lyrically, it is more inward looking than Death Metal, with themes of depression, despair and addiction added to the usual gore and mutilation.

This genre was particularly popular in Finland, where such bands as **Shape Of Despair** and **Unholy** perfected the overwhelming atmosphere of doom and dismay that is characteristic of the style.

Pagan Angel formed in 1990 in Liverpool, England, then reinvented themselves as **Anathema** for the 1994 album *Serenades*. Over the years they have moved away from Doom Metal towards a more melodic and mainstream form of metal music.

Hamferd, from the Faroe Islands, formed in 2008 and released their debut album *Evst* in 2013. Obviously in no big hurry, they released the follow-up *Támsins Likam* in 2018. This band brings pastoral themes and folk textures to the Doom Metal genre.

Other noted exponents of the style include **Crowbar** and **Acid Bath** from New Orleans, **The Obsessed** and **Internal Void** from Virginia, **Witch Mountain**, and **Red Fang** from Oregon.

Above, Right: Vincent Cavanagh of British Doom/Gothic Metal band **Anathema**. The band includes three Cavanagh brothers and two Douglas brothers.

Opposite, Inset: Sludge Metal/Doom Metal **Crowbar** come from New Orleans and have had many different band members.

Opposite: Jón Aldará vocalist with the Faroese Doom Metal band **Hamferð (Hamferd)** performing at the Faroese music festival G! Festival in the Faroe Islands, July 2014.

EXTREME METAL

This is essentially an umbrella term for all of the darker forms of metal, including Black Metal, Death Metal, Doom Metal, Thrash Metal, and Speed Metal. In general, these bands draw on Hardcore Punk as an influence, as well as the classic 1970s metal influences (**Black Sabbath**, **Deep Purple**) and the stripped down hard rock of **Motörhead**. The 1982 album *Reign In Blood* by California band **Slayer** is often cited as the first (and best) Extreme Metal album to appear. Around the same time Swiss band **Celtic Frost** were making a big impact on many European teens who were soon to form their own bands and inspire the Extreme Metal scene to explode.

Extreme Metal is a term often applied to those bands that defy the more rigid definitions of other metal genres. **Strapping Young Lad** from Canada is a good example. Their leader, Devin Townsend, made the first recordings by himself with a drum machine, later recruiting musicians to form a band. Although the musical characteristics of albums like debut *Heavy As A Really Heavy Thing* align with the fast riffing, tempo changes, and percussive assault of other Extreme Metal releases, the sheer eccentricity of Townsend made it difficult to pigeonhole his output.

Main Photo: Strapping Young Lad, were a Canadian band founded in 1996 by Devin Townsend as a one-man studio project. After recruiting a band and five studio albums, they folded in May 2007 with Townsend retreating into the studio to record solo albums. Seen at Dynamo Open Air festival, Weert, Netherlands, July 2002.

Right: Australian band **Deströyer 666** was founded in Melbourne in 1994 as an Extreme Metal solo venture by K.K. Warslut, but soon developed into a three-piece band.

Main Photo: Anna Murphy of **Eluveitie**—she plays the hurdy-gurdy and flute. Formed in 2002 in Switzerland with Murphy joining in 2006, **Eluveitie** uses guitars and traditional instruments with lyrics in harsh vocals often in Gaulish, an extinct language.

Opposite, Left: Mikael Karlbom of **Finntroll** at Bloodstock in August 2011.

Opposite, Right: Gavin Harper of Scottish Folk Metal **Alestorm**, (formed 2004) in June 2008. They riff on a pirate theme—hence the term Pirate Metal!

FOLK METAL

Folk metal is a sub-genre that developed in Europe during the 1990s. As the name suggests, the genre is a fusion of Heavy Metal with traditional folk music. This includes the widespread use of folk instruments and, to a lesser extent, traditional singing styles.

The earliest exponent of Folk Metal was the English band **Skyclad**. Their debut album *The Wayward Sons of Mother Earth* was released in 1990. It was not until 1994 and 1995 that other early contributors in the genre began to emerge from different regions of Europe as well as in Israel. Among these early groups, the Irish band **Cruachan** and the German band **Subway to Sally** each spearheaded a different regional variation that over time became known as Celtic Metal and Medieval Metal respectively. Despite their contributions, Folk Metal remained little known with few representatives during the 1990s. It was not until the early 2000s when the genre exploded into prominence, particularly in Finland with the efforts of such groups as **Finntroll**, **Ensiferum**, **Korpiklaani**, **Turisas**, and **Moonsorrow**.

The music of Folk Metal is characterized by its diversity with bands known to perform different styles of both Heavy Metal music and folk music. A large variety of folk instruments are used in the genre, with many bands consequently featuring six or more members in their regular line-ups. A few bands are also known to rely on keyboards to simulate the sound of folk instruments. Lyrics in the genre commonly deal with paganism, nature, fantasy, mythology, and history.

FUNK METAL

In the late 1960s and early 1970s, heavy bands were also allowed to be funky. Outfits like the **James Gang** and **The Edgar Winter Band** blended their heavy rock and blues influences with a touch of modern rhythm and blues, but as the decade progressed hard rock became less rhythmically adventurous … until the 1980s, when some of the Alternative Metal bands emerging from Hardcore and Post Punk let their funk flag fly once more.

The most successful of these bands by far was **The Red Hot Chili Peppers**. Their 1984 debut release is widely thought to be the first of this genre, and their popularity peaked in 1991 with the Rick Rubin-produced *Blood Sugar Sex Magic*. Other contemporaries included **Faith No More** and **Fishbone**. In the 1990s, **Rage Against The Machine** took the sound to a new level with the excellent guitar innovations of Tom Morello.

By the 2000s, the genre was widely thought to be played out. **The Red Hot Chili Peppers** went in a more melodic direction with their album *Californication*. **Rage Against The Machine** vocalist Zack de la Rocha left, and the band reformed as **Audioslave** with vocalist Chris Cornell. Although popular, **Audioslave** were a much less confrontational band, and decidedly less funky.

Opposite: Guitarist Tom Morello of **Rage Against The Machine**. They started in Los Angeles in 1987 and pursued a committed Leftist agenda; after four studio albums and significant critical and commercial success, they folded in 2011. Here at the Ford Theatre in September 2014 in Hollywood, CA.

Below, Left: The Flea (Michael Balzary) of the **Red Hot Chili Peppers**, in 2016. He has been with them since inception in 1984, but has played with numerous other acts as well as having a successful acting career in tv and the movies.

Below, Right: Tim Commerford, Zack De La Rocha, and Brad Wilk of **Rage Against the Machine** at the 2011 L.A. Rising Music Festival on July 30, 2011 in Los Angeles, CA.

GLAM METAL

Glam Metal evolved from the early 1970s Glam Rock movement epitomized in the USA by **Alice Cooper**, **Kiss**, **Twisted Sister**, and the **New York Dolls**. In 1978, Los Angeles band **Van Halen** emerged with a flashy new guitar technique known as "tapping" and although not strictly a glam band, apart from lead singer David Lee Roth, they greatly influenced the Sunset Strip music scene that burgeoned in the early 1980s.

Musically, Glam Metal pushed the 1970s metal sound into unashamedly pop territory. The flashy soloing is combined with pop riffing and catchy choruses with vocal harmonies. This genre perfected the "power ballad": slower songs with grandiose arrangements and romantic lyrical themes ("for the chicks"), adding enormously to mainstream acceptance and massive sales.

MTV-friendly **Mötley Crüe's** 1981 debut *Too Fast For Love* was arguably the first true Glam Metal release. In 1983, the album *Metal Health* by **Quiet Riot** was first of its type to reach number one on the *Billboard* chart. Pennsylvania band **Poison** had enormous success in the late 1980s, selling over forty-five million records worldwide

In the 1990s, the advent of Grunge hastened the eclipse of Glam Metal, but in recent years such bands as the UK's **The Darkness** have helped bring about something of a revival.

Main Photo: Black Veil Brides, on the 2011 Warped Tour. They are inspired by 1980s era Glam Metal acts.

Left: The very epitome of Hair Metal—**Poison**—on stage during a 1987 Long Beach, CA, gig. They hit the big time soon after founding in 1983 and enjoyed a decade of success. They are still performing and recording.

Main Photo: Peter Steele of **Type O Negative** in May 1997 in Eindhoven, Netherlands. They formed in New York in 1989 and folded in 2010 following Steele's untimely death.

Above: Paradise Lost formed in 1988 and are often referred to as pioneers of Gothic Metal. Their only line-up changes have been the drummers. Shown here at Barcelona Metal Fest in July 2014.

Above, Right: Cristina Scabbia is one of two lead singers for **Lacuna Coil**, (the other is Andrea Ferro). Seen here during the River City RockFest in May 2014 in San Antonio, TX.

GOTHIC METAL

Gothic Metal combines the Goth rock characteristics of 1980s bands like **Sisters Of Mercy** with the heavy riffing of metal music. It might fairly be seen as one of the more "feminine" metal genres, eschewing as it does the more macho trappings in favor of atmospheric backdrops and inward-searching lyrics. It's also responsible for something called the "beauty and the beast" style in which female vocals are contrasted with the guttural male vocals characteristic of Black and Doom Metal.

Iconic UK band **Black Sabbath** were one of the first successful bands to incorporate gothic imagery into their music. US band **Blue Öyster Cult** also used gothic imagery in such songs as cowbell-drenched "Don't Fear The Reaper." It was the UK New Wave scene of the late 1970s and early 1980s, however, that really led to an explosion of Goth type music. Early Goth pioneers **Siouxsie And The Banshees** and **The Cure** set the tone, and later bands **Sisters Of Mercy** and **Fields Of The Nephilim**, incorporated heavy riffing and other metal influences.

UK band **Paradise Lost** formed in 1988 and released their first album *Lost Paradise* in 1990. They were one of three bands who emerged from the North of England at around the same time with the same Goth outlook, the others being **My Dying Bride** and **Anathema**.

GRINDCORE

This is a unique and principally DIY genre, which has its roots in the self-released experiments of punk and new wave bands in the late 1970s. Grindcore albums are often passed around as tapes or CDRs amongst like-minded fans instead of being released through the usual channels. Grindcore uses many of the musical tropes of Hardcore Punk and Thrash Metal but differs in execution: songs may run at speeds of 190 beats/minute or more, they may—or may not—include vocals, and they might be very short. A Grindcore "microsong" can be over in a couple of seconds, and even the more traditional songs are often ninety seconds or less in length.

UK band **Napalm Death** is often cited as the principal originator of the genre and has an entry in the *Guinness Book Of Records* for shortest ever song: the catchy "You Suffer" clocks in at a mere 1.316 seconds!

North America subsequently took the genre to heart with such picturesquely named bands as **Cripple Bastards** and **Assück**.

Swedish Grindcore band **Birdflesh** add humor and theatricality to the mix and this has made their live act popular at such Grindcore-centric festivals as the Obscene Extreme World Tour, a globe-trotting event.

Above, Right: Founded in December 1986 in the English Midlands, no original members of **Napalm Death** are still with the band—but they are still seen as pioneers of Grindcore. Seventeen departed band members later (they are currently a four-piece), they have nevertheless managed to release fifteen studio albums.

Right: Gutalax formed in the Czech Republic in 2009. They are popular in underground grime circles but have yet to break out into the wider Extreme Metal audience.

Opposite: Although a New Yorker, Mitch Harris has played guitar and sung back-up vocals for Midlands, England-based, **Napalm Death** since 1989.

Right: Mike Spreitzer of **Devil Driver** at Ritz Manchester in March 2013 in Manchester, England. Founded in Santa Barbera, CA in 2002, as of 2014 they are in hiatus.

GROOVE METAL

Groove Metal utilizes "dance tempos," generally 115 to 135 beats/minute, and this distinguishes it from other genres like the super fast Grindcore or the super slow Doom Metal. In 1990, Texas band **Pantera** released its debut *Cowboys From Hell* and band members themselves coined the term Groove Metal to describe their music.

In 2000, Virginia band **Lamb Of God** released breakthrough album *New American Gospel* and were immediately hailed as the "Future of Metal" by some reviewers. They certainly hit on a winning formula, combining the groove-tempo riffs of **Pantera** with a deft feel for the production advances of the 1990s. In 2006, their album *Sacrament* hit number eight on the *Billboard Hot 200* chart.

California band **Devil Driver** released their eponymous debut album in 2003. It wasn't very well received, and their 2005 follow up *The Fury Of Our Maker's Hand* has been called their "true" debut. The band plays a kind of Death Metal with Groove Metal tempos.

Other Groove Metal bands include **Machine Head**, **White Zombie**, **Texas Hippie Coalition**, and **Five Finger Death Punch** (aka **5FDP**).

Opposite: Randy Blythe of **Lamb of God** (aka **LoG**) at The Egyptian Room at Old National Centre in November 2012 in Indianapolis, IN. Founded in 1994 in Richmond, VA., their lyrical themes include politics, apocalyptic themes, and anti-religious sentiment.

Right: From Marseille, France, **Dagoba** were formed in 1998 by their lead vocalist Shawter. To date they have released seven studio albums despite frequent changes in their ranks.

Main photo: Co-founder and lead guitarist Jerry Cantrell of **Alice In Chains** during their 2013 concert tour. Founded in the late 1980s, they play a distinctive mix of acoustic and heavy metal. They have sold around thirty-five million albums worldwide.

Opposite: Soundgarden from Seattle were the first grunge band to sign for a major record label. They finally found success in the 1990s but broke up in 1997. They reformed in 2010 since when they have been successfully operating.

GRUNGE

Grunge began in the Pacific Northwest of the United States, and was initially a reaction against the polished and commercialized Glam Metal that dominated MTV in the 1980s. However, if there is a genre title that is universally despised by those it supposedly represents, this is the one. It was primarily a word used by music journalists to describe a certain type of guitar distortion. In the mid-1980s, there was a thriving Australian scene known as "Grunge," a legacy of classic local punk band **The Saints**.

The music that emerged from Seattle in the late 1980s to early 1990s ranged in style from punk to classic metal, but the one thing that characterized all of it was a strong adherence to melody. This trait helped Grunge bands, in particular **Nirvana**, to achieve success beyond their wildest dreams. The consequences of this were all too often tragic. Before too long the term fell out of favor, a victim of its own success.

Pearl Jam was one of the more mainstream of the Grunge bands, with a multi-platinum debut album, *Ten*. **Soundgarden** was another band that achieved success with its melodic brand of classic rock. Elsewhere, but still in Seattle, **Alice In Chains** had a unique and arresting blend of acoustic guitars, heavy riffs, and eerie vocals.

HARDCORE PUNK

Main Photo: Tim McIlrath (seen here at Leeds Festival) and Joe Principe are the only remaining original members of **Rise Against** from their formation in Chicago in 1999. They are described as Melodic Hardcore and are particularly committed to animal welfare rights and progressive orginazations for political change.

Left: Frontman Tim Williams (center) and guitarist Matt Baumbach of American Hardcore Punk **Vision Of Disorder** performing aboard HMS *Hammer* en route to the Golden Gods Awards in London, in June 2013.

Below, Left: Harley Flanagan with American Hardcore Thrash Punk band **Cro-Mags** at Metro in Chicago, IL, in March 1987.

In the early 1980s, Punk Rock took hold in the USA with a sound that was harder and higher in tempo. The suburban youth that made it had no time for the art school pretensions of the early punks and the post punks. They wanted to forge a scene that was truly inclusive to all, with a stripped down music and attitude that soon became known as "Hardcore."

Early 1980s pioneers included Los Angeles band **Black Flag**, **The Dead Kennedys** from San Francisco, and **Bad Brains** from Washington DC. Soon there were Hardcore Punk bands from every place in between: **Husker Dü** in Minneapolis, **Meat Puppets** in Arizona. Texas had its **Butthole Surfers**. Over in the UK, Sheffield spawned **Discharge** and Scotland had **The Expoited**.

New York bands **Cro-Mags** and **Vision Of Disorder** allowed more traditional Heavy Metal influences into their music. **Cro-Mags**' debut *The Age of Quarrel* was released in 1986 and was highly influential. **Vision Of Disorder** released their self-titled debut ten years later, upping the stakes in terms of melodic sense and polished production. Chicago's **Rise Against** recorded three platinum albums for Geffen Records in the 2000s.

INDUSTRIAL METAL

Industrial Music was a "New Wave" genre birthed in the late 1970s by a variety of bands from the UK and the USA including **Throbbing Gristle**, **This Heat**, **Cabaret Voltaire**, **Chrome**, and **Z'ev**. These bands played a confrontational type of experimental music, heavily influenced by the early 1970s releases of such bands as Germany's **Faust**, **Can**, and **Kraftwerk**, and the "cut-up" technique of author William Burroughs. In the 1980s, the sound and attitude evolved into a fascinating variety of "micro scenes." **Laibach** in Slovenia, **Swans** in New York, **DAF** in Germany, and **Young Gods** in Switzerland are just four examples of bands that forged a unique identity through a combination of music, art, and uncompromising live performance. In the late 1980s, bands such as **Rammstein** began to synthesize these styles into a new form of Heavy Metal.

American bands **Nine Inch Nails**, **Ministry**, and **Marilyn Manson** sold millions of units in the 1990s with their blend of industrial, metal, and pop. By the turn of the century, although the core players continued to do good work, the term "Industrial" had largely fallen out of favor.

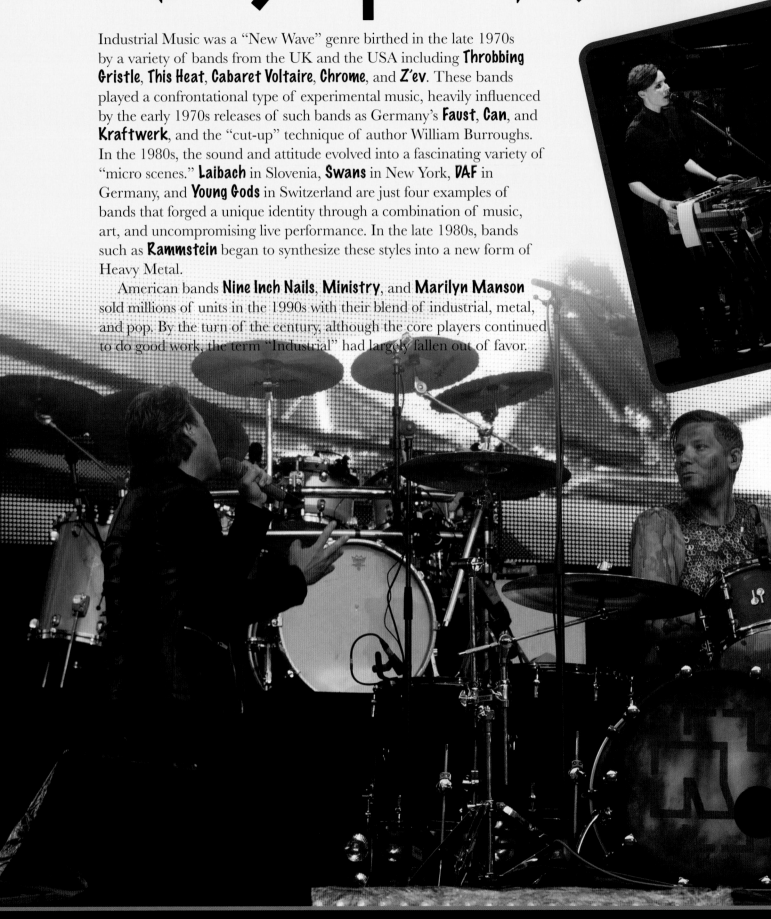

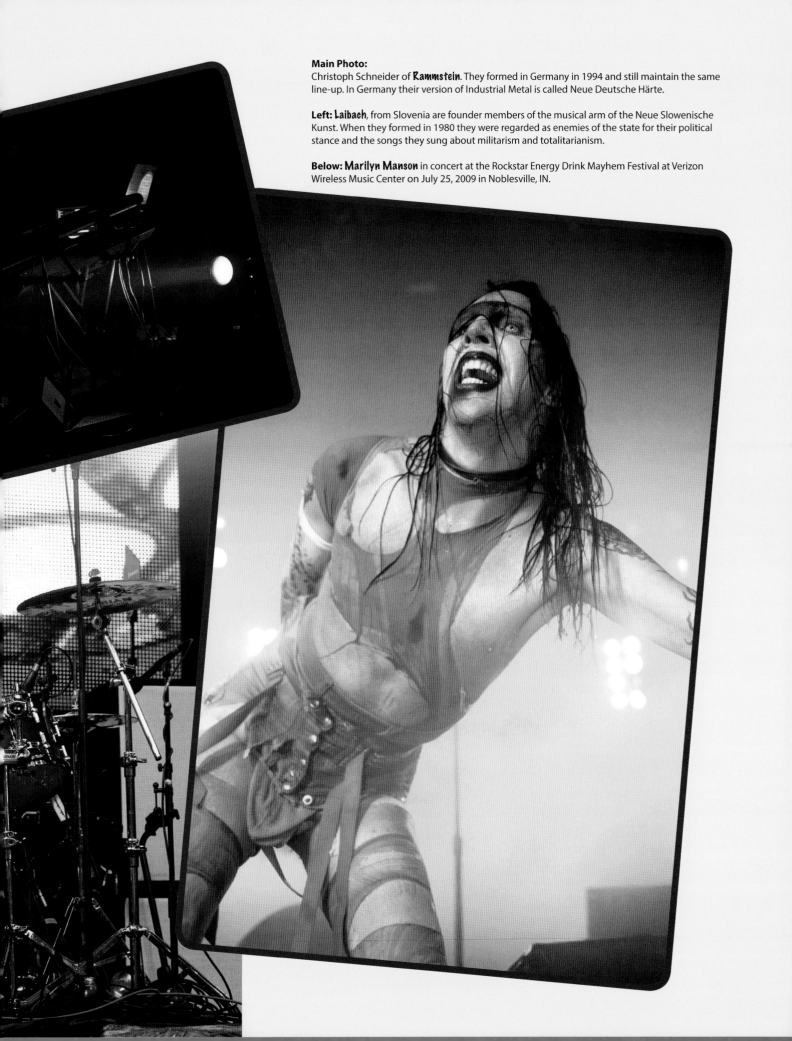

Main Photo:
Christoph Schneider of **Rammstein**. They formed in Germany in 1994 and still maintain the same line-up. In Germany their version of Industrial Metal is called Neue Deutsche Härte.

Left: Laibach, from Slovenia are founder members of the musical arm of the Neue Slowenische Kunst. When they formed in 1980 they were regarded as enemies of the state for their political stance and the songs they sung about militarism and totalitarianism.

Below: Marilyn Manson in concert at the Rockstar Energy Drink Mayhem Festival at Verizon Wireless Music Center on July 25, 2009 in Noblesville, IN.

METALCORE

Metalcore is a blend of Hardcore Punk and Alternative Metal. It arose in the mid-1980s as Hardcore Punk bands evolved and began to take on a bigger variety of influences. New York band **Cro-Mags**' 1986 debut album *The Age Of Quarrel* was an early example, and by the 1990s, there were numerous Metalcore bands all over the world. Metalcore shares the political attitude and inclusivity of Hardcore Punk.

New York's **Earth Crisis** formed in 1989 and released debut *Destroy The Machines* in 1995. They are considered one of the earlier Metalcore bands, with a sound that was more Hardcore Punk than metal. Later bands of the genre were more inclined towards their metal influences with slower tempos and "breakdowns" aimed at maximum mosh pit efficacy.

The Dillinger Escape Plan released their debut *Calculating Infinity* in 1999. They are sometimes referred to as "Mathcore" for the occasional complexity of their music, as are the UK's **Rolo Tomassi**, who formed in 2005. Boston's **Ice Nine Kills** even included ska influences in their early music before evolving in a more Neoclassical direction.

Opposite, Above: Attack Attack! at a Halloween costume concert at The Emerson Theater in October 2012 in Indianapolis, IN. They disbanded the following year.

Opposite, Below: Jeff Tuttle (R) of **The Dillinger Escape Plan** joins Bryan Kienlen of the **Bouncing Souls** at the Time Warner Cable Amphitheater at Tower City in July 2010 in Cleveland, OH.

Left: Guitarist Matthieu Murphy of the Metalcore band **Tear Out The Heart** performs on stage at The Emerson Theater in February 2014. They formed in 2011 in St Louis, MO.

Below: Eva Spence of English Metalcore/Mathcore band **Rolo Tomassi** on the second day of Heavy Music Festival at Port Lympne Wild Animal Park in August 2010 in Lympne, England.

NEOCLASSICAL METAL

Main Photo: Classically trained cellists Perttu Kivilaakso, Eicca Toppinen, and Paavo Loetjoenen of **Apocalyptica** are all graduates of the Sibelius Academy, Helsinki, Finland. Shown during a gig at the Tempodrom in March 2014, in Berlin, Germany.

Left: Perttu Kivilaakso of Finnish Neoclassical/Symphonic Metal band **Apocalyptica** on stage during the Rock On The Range festival at Crew Stadium in May 2010 in Columbus, OH.

Opposite: Malmsteen is the eponymous band of Yngwie Malmsteen (born Lars Johan Yngve Lannerbäck) the Swedish musician-songwriter known for his neo-classical Heavy Metal guitar playing. On stage at Bikini in June 2005 in Barcelona, Spain.

This style of metal goes way back to 1969 with the release during that year of the Deep Purple album *Concerto For Group And Orchestra*. In 1976, Ritchie Blackmore and his band **Rainbow** released the popular album *Rising* which featured the Munich Symphony Orchestra. In the late 1970s, Eddie Van Halen perfected the "tapping" style almost universally adopted by Neoclassical Metal guitarists.

It was Swedish guitar maestro Yangwie Malmsteen who brought the style into the mainstream in the 1980s. He released his first solo album *Rising Force* in 1984 and received a Grammy nomination for Best Rock Instrumental. He is still active and was part of Steve Vai's Generation Axe Tour in 2016.

Apocalyptica from Finland formed in 1993 when the then college friends gathered to play **Metallica** covers, a project that would subsequently become their first album *Apocalyptica Plays Metallica By Four Cellos*. By the early 2000s, their albums were mostly original material.

"Cello Metal" notwithstanding, Neoclassical Metal is a predominately guitar-based genre, largely confined to those players skilled enough to trot out super-fast arpeggio runs. In recent years, **Symphony X**, **Rhapsody of Fire**, **Trans Siberian Orchestra**, and **Stratovarius** have released popular albums.

What was originally called Alternative Metal gradually became known as Nu Metal: a conglomeration of styles with a Heavy Metal underpinning. The styles included Industrial, Funk, Hip Hop, and Hardcore. It was such 1990s bands as **Limp Bizkit** and **Korn** who really personified this genre. These bands were too mainstream to be labeled "Alternative Metal," and thus a new term was coined.

Nu Metal combines the "danceable" mid tempos of Groove Metal with Hip Hop elements (particularly turntable effects and rapping), and lyrics that could be defined as "emo" (dealing with personal issues), a strong melodic or pop element, and a comparative lack of guitar pyrotechnics.

Korn's eponymous 1994 debut album is often cited as the first major Nu Metal release. **Limp Bizkit's** debut was released three years later. In the late 1990s, a series of sexual harassment incidents at **Limp Bizkit** gigs put a blight on their career.

In the 2000s, **Linkin Park** from California and Des Moines, Iowa natives **Slipknot** rose to prominence. **Linkin Park** have been multi-platinum sellers from their 2000 debut *Hybrid Theory*. They released their seventh album *One More Light* in 2017. Sadly their singer Chester Bennington committed suicide a few weeks later.

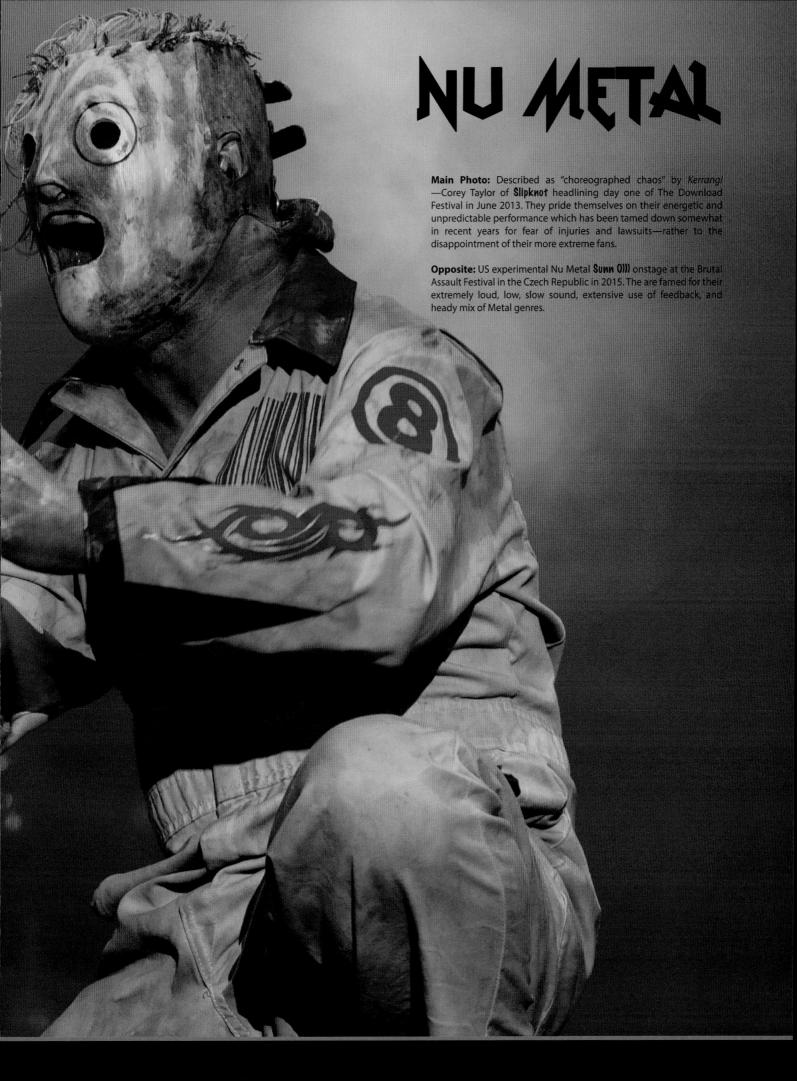

NU METAL

Main Photo: Described as "choreographed chaos" by *Kerrang!* —Corey Taylor of **Slipknot** headlining day one of The Download Festival in June 2013. They pride themselves on their energetic and unpredictable performance which has been tamed down somewhat in recent years for fear of injuries and lawsuits—rather to the disappointment of their more extreme fans.

Opposite: US experimental Nu Metal **Sunn O)))** onstage at the Brutal Assault Festival in the Czech Republic in 2015. The are famed for their extremely loud, low, slow sound, extensive use of feedback, and heady mix of Metal genres.

POST-METAL

In the 1990s, a number of bands including US band **Tortoise** and Scottish outfit **Mogwai** were classified as "Post Rock." Inevitably a subgenre came into being to include bands that were deemed Post Rock but were still metal bands at their core. Thus Post Metal was born.

The seeds had already been sown in the 1980s by bands such as Seattle's **The Melvins**, who pushed the textural boundaries of metal music into strange new shapes. In New York, bands like **Sonic Youth** and **Swans** were combining metal riffs with new sonic textures.

Neurosis was one of the first metal bands to be termed Post Metal with its third album *Souls At Zero* in 1992. The same year, UK band **Godflesh** released its second album *Pure*. These two albums form the foundation of the Post Metal genre.

Swedish Post Metal band **Cult Of Luna** formed in 1998 and released several albums before going on hiatus in 2006. In 2016, they released their seventh album *Mariner*, adding US vocalist Julie Christmas to their lineup.

San Francisco band **Deafheaven** released a popular debut with *Roads To Judah* in 2011, and their 2013 follow-up *Sunbather* achieved wide acclaim.

Opposite: Johannes Persson of Swedish **Cult of Luna** onstage at The Garage, January 22, 2013. They went on hiatus soon afterwards and intend to return "in one form or another."

Right: Scott Kelly (L) and Dave Edwardson of **Neurosis** at High Voltage Festival, in London, July 2011. Originally formed in 1985 in Oakland CA as a Hardcore Punk band they have changed style over the years to play influential Post-Metal music.

POWER METAL

This is an epic-themed and pop-honed genre, and also perhaps the most faithful to the "roots of metal." It combines a sword-and-sorcery approach to lyric writing with high-pitched vocal delivery and anthem-like choruses. British bands **Iron Maiden** and **Judas Priest** had a lot of influence on the musical style of Power Metal.

Germany's **Helloween**, formed in 1984, were seen as early pioneers of the genre. Albums *Keeper Of The Seven Keys I and II* (1987 and 1989) still top many lists of best Power Metal albums.

As the 1990s progressed, two distinct types of Power Metal emerged: US and European styles. US bands adopted more of a Speed or Thrash Metal approach and use of keyboards was rare. Across the Atlantic, European bands allowed more "prog" influences with keyboards and arrangements that were less aggressive in tone.

US Power Metal band, **The Omen** formed in 1983 and released their first major label album *The Curse* on Capitol Records in 1986 and had a hit single in 1988 with "Thorn In Your Flesh."

UK band **DragonForce** is typical of the European approach to Power Metal, using keyboards and electronic textures, even evoking early video game soundtracks.

Left: Floor Jansen and Marco Hietala of **Nightwish** in October 2012 in Anaheim, CA. Despite being Finnish the band sings predominently in English.

Opposite, Above: Marcus Siepen and Oliver Holzwarth of **Blind Guardian**. The band emerged from the German Heavy Metal scene in 1984 as **Lucifer's Heritage** and played under that name until 1988.

Opposite, Below: Londoners Herman Li and Sam Totman (both ex **Demoniac**) playing their high speed dual guitars that give **Dragonforce** its distinctive sound. Onstage during day one of The Download Festival in June 2013 .

PROGRESSIVE METAL

Progressive Metal is another genre built on the traditional metal sound, with added elements influenced by the progressive rock bands of the 1970s. By far the best of these bands was the UK's **King Crimson**, led by guitar maestro Robert Fripp. Canadian band **Rush**, who formed in 1968, pioneered a combination of Metal and Prog that was also highly influential.

Three American bands rose to prominence in the 1980s and are crucial to the development of Progressive Metal: **Queensrÿche** from Washington, **Fates Warning** from Connecticut, and **Dream Theater** from Massachusetts. **Queensrÿche** formed in 1982 and had two massive hit albums with *Operation: Mindcrime* (1988) and *Empire* (1990). **Fates Warning** and **Dream Theater** have also sold millions of albums worldwide.

The most basic requirement of Progressive Metal, as with Prog Rock before it, is a high level of musical virtuosity. This level was upped even further with the emergence of the "djent" technique, a form of insanely fast muted and tapped arpeggio playing. This was pioneered by Swedish band **Meshuggah** and the UK's **SikTh**. UK composer/instrumentalist Paul Ortiz, (who records as **Chimp Spanner**) is also a leading practitioner of the style.

Main Photo: Trans-Siberian Orchestra on in Greenville, SC in November 2013. Celebrated for their series of rock operas, they are in the top ten ticket-selling bands on the current music scene.

Below, Left: Composer and musician Paul Ortiz uses the name **Chimp Spanner** for his Progressive Metal/djent solo projects. When playing live he is accompanied by Jim Hughes (guitar), Adam Swan (bass), and Boris Le Gal (drums). Shown on stage in September 2011 in Sheffield, England.

Opposite, Left: English musicians Dan Weller (L) and Graham "Pin" Pinney, guitarists with progressive metal group **SikTh**, photographed in London in March 2014. Along with **Meshuggah** they are leaders of the djent movement.

Opposite, Right: The grandfather of Progressive Metal, Mr **King Crimson**, Robert Fripp, as seen in 1973. His innovative musicianship has been the backbone of his over four decades long career in the music business, during which time he has collaborated with many of the greatest names in rock music.

RAP METAL

In the mid-1980s, several Hip Hop acts sampled rock and metal riffs, notably **Run DMC**, whose collaboration with US rock band **Aerosmith** "Walk This Way" was highly influential. **Beastie Boys**, **Cypress Hill**, and **Public Enemy** all used metal riffs in their songs. Rapper **Ice T** formed his own pioneering Rap Metal band, **Body Count**, in 1990. Conversely, metal band **Anthrax** released rapping single "I'm The Man" in 1987—this was for many the true birth of the Rap Metal genre.

In the 1990s, Rap Metal went mainstream with the success of such bands as **Rage Against The Machine** and **Kid Rock**. Although **Rage Against The Machine** was a hugely popular band and sold millions of units, **Kid Rock** was more typical of the macho and partying preoccupations of most Rap Metal bands. **Faith No More** had their own Rap Metal hit with "Epic."

Papa Roach, from Vacaville, CA, had a triple-platinum hit with their debut album *Infest* in 2000. The band played Ozzfest in 2001 and went from strength to strength. Their decision to drop the rap element of their music reflects a general movement of many bands away from the genre.

Opposite: Jacoby Shaddix of Papa Roach during the Louder Than Life Music Festival in Champions Park, October 2014 in Louisville, KY. Founded in 1993, the band has had huge success, but in recent years has moved away from rapping.

Above: Faith No More in 1990 during The Real Thing Tour. These were their first gigs with new singer Mike Patton.

Right: P.O.D. (aka Payable on Death) are a Christian Rap Metal band founded in 1992 in San Diago, CA. They have moved on from rap to a reggae influenced Alternative Metal style. Seen here at Live 105's BFD at Shoreline Amphitheater in Mountain View, CA in June 2000.

SLUDGE METAL

This largely down-tempo genre blends elements of Doom Metal with the shouted and screamed vocals of Hardcore Punk, and has its roots in early **Black Sabbath**. Other bands that influenced the style include **Swans** from New York (in particular their 1984 album *Cop*) and **The Melvins** from Washington.

The Melvins' 1987 debut album *Gluey Porch Treatments* is generally regarded as a pioneering record of the Sludge Metal genre. This Seattle-based band would go on to have a big influence on that city's Grunge movement.

In New Orleans, LA a significant Sludge Metal scene developed, featuring such bands as **Eyehategod**, **Crowbar**, and **Acid Bath**. On the East Coast, Boston band **Grief** combined a tortuous sludgy grind with bellowed emo lyrics.

Mastodon formed in Atlanta, GA in 2000 and released their debut album *Remission* in 2002. Although their early work could be termed Sludge Metal they have become one of the most critically respected metal bands of recent years.

Mouth Of The Architect from Dayton, OH, released their debut album *Time And Withering* in 2004. They have released five albums to date, the most recent being *Path Of Eight* in 2016.

Main Photo: Brent Hinds of **Mastodon** in front of the crowd on day two of the Roskilde Festival in July 2011.

Opposite, Left: Steve Brooks (L) and Joe Lester of US Atmospheric Sludge Metal **Mouth of the Architect**. Live at The Croft, May 2010.

Opposite, Right: Buzz Osborne of **The Melvins** on stage at All Tomorrows Parties Festival, May 2012. They usually perform as a trio but have recently added a second drummer.

SPEED METAL

Speed Metal is commonly held to have evolved from the New Wave of British Heavy Metal (usually referred to by the catchy acronym NWOBHM), a late1970s to early 1980s movement that was spearheaded by the stripped-down rock of Lemmy's **Motörhead**. This type of metal is less bluesy, the tempo is faster, and punk influences are allowed. The genre is generally thought to have helped birth the subsequent more extreme styles of metal.

Before **Motörhead**, however, there was **Deep Purple**. Their song "Speed King" exemplified the fast and precise playing employed by Speed Metal and arguably this one song birthed the whole genre.

Anvil formed in 1981 in Canada. Their early albums had a big influence on emerging bands like **Metallica**. Even after obscurity beckoned they soldiered on, eventually enjoying a renaissance in 2008 with the "rockumetary" *Anvil! The Story of Anvil*.

Ultimately, Speed Metal evolved into Thrash Metal, a less technically demanding genre. Some bands, however, continued to fly the flag. Finland's **Thunderstone**, led by Speed Metal maestro Nino Laurenne, formed in 2000 and had a lot of success with albums like *Tools of Destruction* (2005).

Main photo: Sharon den Adel in June 2014 with Dutch Metal **Within Temptation** live at Copenhell in Copenhagen. They have become considerably more melodic since their Goth Metal inception in 1996.

Right: Italian Symphonic Power Metal **Rhapsody of Fire** live in Rome. In an amicable split in 2011, three members of the band left to become **Luca Turilli's Rhapsody**, a complimentary parallel band.

Below: Ross White and Mark Harrington of **Pythia** in April 2013 in Manchester. Formed in London in 2007, they sing of the supernatural and dark stories of mystery.

Opposite, Inset: Operatic vocalist Floor Jansen with **Nightwish** at Shepherd's Bush Empire in London, November 2012. Many of their songs are highly personal and emotional.

Symphonic Metal combines a modern metal sound with orchestral elements. Vocals are operatic in style and often performed by female sopranos, as is the case with Floor Jansen of prime exponents **Nightwish**. Of course, orchestras being expensive, Symphonic Metal bands often use keyboards to replicate orchestras and choirs in their arrangements. Lyrical themes generally follow the fantasy or "sword and sorcery" playbook.

Pennsylvania Christian Metal band **Believer** is commonly held to have sowed the seed for Symphonic Metal with 1990 song "Dies Irae." Swedish band **Therion**, who started as Death Metal, gradually added more symphonic elements to their sound; they had a big influence on Finnish band **Nightwish**, who released their first album *Angels Fall First* in 1997. **Within Temptation** from the Netherlands released their debut *Enter* the same year and also have an operatic female vocalist in Sharon den Adel.

Italian band **Rhapsody of Fire** released a series of albums between 1997 and 2011 that told its own fantasy saga. They then split into two different but complementary bands, **Rhapsody** and **Luca Turilli's Rhapsody**.

London-based **Pythia** released their debut *Beneath The Veiled Embrace* in 2009. In 2015 founding member, vocalist, and former member of **Mediæval Bæbes**, Emily Alice Ovenden, left and was replaced by Sophie Dorman.

SYMPHONIC METAL

THRASH METAL

Thrash Metal is a sub-genre of Heavy Metal that is characterized most typically by its fast tempo and aggression. Thrash Metal songs typically use fast percussive beats and fast, low-register guitar riffs, overlaid with shredding-style lead work. Lyrically, Thrash Metal songs often deal with social issues and reproach the establishment, often using direct and denunciatory language, an approach which partially overlaps with the hardcore genre.

Thrash metal's "Big Four," the four bands widely regarded as the genre's most successful and influential acts, are **Metallica**, **Slayer**, **Megadeth**, and **Anthrax** due to their status as pioneers of the genre in the 1980s. Some common characteristics of Thrash Metal are fast guitar riffs with aggressive picking styles and fast guitar solos, and extensive use of two bass drums as opposed to the conventional use of only one, typical of most rock music.

The origins of Thrash Metal are generally traced to the late 1970s and early 1980s, when a number of predominantly American bands began fusing elements of the new wave of British Heavy Metal with the speed and aggression of Hardcore Punk. Thrash Metal is more aggressive compared to its relative, Speed Metal, and is thought to have emerged at least in part as a reaction to the more conventional and widely acceptable (ie, popular) sounds and themes of Glam Metal, a less aggressive, pop music-infused, Heavy Metal sub-genre which emerged simultaneously.

Main Photo: Metallica's spectacular lightshow at the fifty-sixth Grammy Awards in 2014.

Opposite, Inset Right: Joey Belladonna (L) and Scott Ian of **Anthrax** during the Metal Alliance Tour at The Fillmore, Detroit in April 2013 . . . still going strong after thirty years.

Opposite, Inset Left: Twenty-two-year old singer and arrow axeman James Hetfield of **Metallica** looks decidedly younger in 1985. Metallica had formed four years earlier and were now starting to really make waves.

VIKING METAL

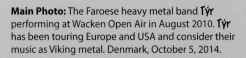

Main Photo: The Faroese heavy metal band **Týr** performing at Wacken Open Air in August 2010. **Týr** has been touring Europe and USA and consider their music as Viking metal. Denmark, October 5, 2014.

Opposite: Hellheim (the name refers to the home of Hel, and the eponymous old Norse goddess who rules the spirits of the dead in the Underworld) is a Viking Black Metal band that began in 1992 from Bergen, Norway.

Viking Metal is a subgenre of Black Metal that arose in Scandinavia, and Norway in particular, in the 1980s and 1990s. Viking Metal blends Black Metal elements with Nordic folk music and lyrical themes of Norse mythology. Viking Metal bands are generally anti-Christian, but pagan rather then satanic.

Sweden's **Bathory** and Denmark's **Mercyful Fate** are two bands often credited with kick starting Black Metal. However, it was the "second wave" of bands such as Norway's **Mayhem** that pioneered the wash of distorted guitar that characterized the Black Metal and subsequently the Viking Metal sound.

Enslaved, also from Norway, released their first album *Vikingligr Veldi* in 1994. Their second album *Frost* was released the same year and was the first to be described by the band members themselves as Viking Metal.

Burzum was the project of Varg Vikernes, who spent fourteen years in prison for murder and arson after instigating church burnings and killing **Mayhem** member Øystein Aarseth.

He was released in 2009 and moved to France with his family.

The sensational church burnings, murders, and suicides that occurred in the Norwegian scene of the 1990s can perhaps be seen as par for the course for a movement that fostered some dodgy attitudes around Nordic racial purity and superiority.

PHOTO CREDITS

GETTY IMAGES
1 Roger Kisby, 2 Josselin Dupont, 7 Neil Lupin, 8 Christie Goodwin, 11 Michael Ochs Archives, 14 Michael Ochs Archives 15TR Michael Putland, 15TL & B Michael Ochs Archives, 16T Express, 17 Leee Black Childers, 18 Keystone, 19T Michael Putland, 19B Andrew Putler, 21 Michael Putland, 24 Michael Putland (both), 25B Richard E. Aaron, 25T Fin Costello/Redferns, 26–27 Fin Costello/Redferns, 26TR Art Zelin, 26TL Paul Welsh/Redferns, 27TR Waring Abbott, 27TL Michael Ochs Archives, 28 Larry Hulst, 29T Richard E. Aaron, 30BL Hulton Archive, 30BR George Wilkes, 30TL GAB Archive, 30TR Fin Costello, 31 Mick Hutson, 36BL & TR Michael Ochs Archives, 36TL Fin Costello, 37 Mick Hutson, 38 WireImage, 39BR & BL Larry Hulst, 39T Stacia Timonere, 40 Marc S Canter, 41BL Michael Uhll, 41BR Pete Cronin, 41T Paul Natkin, 42BL George Rose, 43 Mike Cameron/Redferns, 44 Bob King/Redferns, 45T Larry Hulst, 45B Catherine McGann, 46B Michael Uhll, 47T Martin Philbey, 48B Pete Cronin, 48T Buda Mendes, 49 Michael Ochs Archives, 54T *Metal Hammer* Magazine, 54B Mick Hutson, 55 Christie Goodwin, 56BR Jo Hale, 56T Mick Hutson, 56BL AFP, 57 Tim Mosenfelder, 58 Gary Wolstenholme, 59T Mat Hayward, 59B Krasner/Trebitz, 60B Mick Hutson, 60T Lindsay Brice, 61 Graham Wiltshire, 62

Classic Rock Magazine, 63B Photoshot, 63T George De Sota, 63C Raymond Boyd, 64 Stefan M. Prager, 65B Ralph Notaro, 66T Mick Hutson, 66B Gary Wolstenholme, 67L Ethan Miller, 67R Bob Berg, 68C Naki, 68T Tim Mosenfelder, 68B Waring Abbott, 69 Paul Bergen, 70TR Ethan Miller, 70B Naki, 70TL Mick Hutson, 71T Gary Wolstenholme, 71B *Metal Hammer* Magazine, 72 Mick Hutson, 73T Mick Hutson, 73B Martin Philbey, 74T Jim Steinfeldt, 74B Hayley Madden, 75T Stefan M. Prager, 76BL & BR Naki, 76T *Metal Hammer* Magazine, 77T & B Tim Mosenfelder, 78–79 Alain Benainous, 78B Steve Thorne, 79T Gary Wolstenholme, 80 Ragnar Singsaas, 81 Samuel Dietz, 83T Mick Hutson, 83B Christie Goodwin, 86T *Metal Hammer* Magazine, 86C Bob Berg, 86B Gary Wolstenholme, 88 PYM-CA, 89T *Metal Hammer* Magazine, 89B Scott Legato, 90C Raymond Boyd, 90B Adam Berry, 90T Mat Hayward, 91 Gary Wolstenholme, 92C Ollie Millington, 92T Naki, 92B Frank Hoensch, 93T *Metal Hammer* Magazine, 93B Mark Venema, 94T *Total Guitar* Magazine, 94B Joey Foley, 94C Scott Legato, 95 Christie Goodwin/Redferns, 96 Dave Benett, 97TL *Metal Hammer* Magazine, 98T Gary Wolstenholme 98B Christie Goodwin, 99 Gary Wolstenholme, 100 Gary Wolstenholme, 101T Jeff Hahne, 101C Joey Foley, 101B Gary Wolstenholme, 103 Nigel Crane, 104 Nigel Crane,

105B, Peter Still, 106 Gary Wolstenholme, 107 Gary Wolstenholme, 111 Gary Wolstenholme, 112B Gary Wolstenholme, 112T Steve Thorne, 113 Naki, 115 Naki, 116 Naki, 117T Gary Wolstenholme, 117B Mick Hutson, 118T Joey Foley, 119T Nigel Crane, 120T Gary Wolstenholme, 120B *Metal Hammer* Magazine, 121 *Metal Hammer* Magazine, 122 *Metal Hammer* Magazine, 123B Gary Wolstenholme, 123T Brian Killian, 124 Photoshot, 125T Gary Wolstenholme, 125B Christie Goodwin, 126T & B Gary Wolstenholme, 127T & B Brigitte Engl, 128 Photoshot, 129BR Gary Wolstenholme, 129L *Total Guitar* Magazine, 130B Naki, 131T Gary Wolstenholme, 133 Ollie Millington, 136 Joey Foley, 137B Joey Foley, 137T Pacific Press, 138 Gary Wolstenholme, 139T Bob Berg, 140 Toru Yamanaka, 142 Larry Marano, 143B Scott Legato, 143T Philip Holbrook, 145T Gary Wolstenholme, 146–147 *Metal Hammer* Magazine, 147T Gary Wolstenholme, 148R Ollie Millington, 149T Raymond Boyd, 149B PYMCA/UIG, 150 Didier Messens, 151B *Metal Hammer* Magazine, 152T Scott Legato, 152B Rick Kern, 154T Tim Mosenfelder, 154B Mat Hayward, 155 C. Brandon, 158T Kevin Winter, 158B Jason Davis, 159T Larry Marano, 159B Scott Legato, 160 Gary Wolstenholme, 161T *Metal Hammer* Magazine, 161B Raymond Boyd, 162 Gary Wolstenholme, 163B *Metal Hammer*

Magazine, 165 Scott Legato, 166 madSec, 167T Rene Johnston, 167B Etienne de Malglaive, 168–169 Andrew Benge, 169T Roger Kisby, 170–171 Stefan Hoederath, 170TL Fin Costello, 172–173 Rick Diamond, 174R Joey Foley, 175T Scott Legato, 175B PYMCA, 178 Peter Pakvis, 180 Gary Wolstenholme, 181L Gary Wolstenholme, 182 Michael Tullberg, 185T George Rose, 186T Jordi Vidal, 186B Gary Miller, 187 Paul Bergen, 190B Joey Foley, 190T Gary Wolstenholme, 192 John Leyba, 194–195 Gary Wolstenholme, 194T *Metal Hammer* Magazine, 194B Stacia Timonere, 197R Mick Hutson, 198T & B Joey Foley, 199T Joey Foley, 199B Felix Kunze, 200–201 Frank Hoensch, 200T Joey Foley, 201T Jordi Vidal, 203 Ollie Millington, 204 *Prog* Magazine, 205 *Metal Hammer* Magazine, 206 Noel Vasquez, 208 Gary Wolstenholme, 209TL *Total Guitar* Magazine, 210 Raymond Boyd, 211T Mick Hutson, 211B Tim Mosenfelder, 212–213 Felix Kunze, 213TL *Metal Hammer* Magazine, 213TR *Total Guitar* Magazine, 216B Gary Wolstenholme, 217B *Prog* Magazine, 218 Kevork Djansezian, 218TL Larry Hulst, 218TR Scott Legato

WikiCommons
3 Mdnghtshdw, 16B Heinrich Klaffs, 29B Raph_PH, 33 Grywnn, 36BR Dark Apostrophe, 42BR Alexandre Cardoso, 42T Mdnghtshdw, 46T Cecil, 47B S.Bollmann, 50 S. Bollmann, 65

Dirulove, 75B Andrew Kelly, 87 christian bueno, 97B Jax 0677, 97TR Jonas Rogowski, 98C S. Bollmann, 102 Floris Looijesteijn, 105T InfoZZ, 108–109 Sven Mandel, 108T Fileri, 109T Lrheath, 110B C. Garrett Padilla, 110T Frank Schwichtenberg, 112C Stefan Bollmann, 114T MrPanyGoff, 114B Raph_PH, 118–119 S. Bollmann, 129TR S. Bollmann, 130T Anderson, 131B Frank Schwichtenberg, 139B MisfitGhoul, 141T BiblioteKarin, 141B José Miguel Rosas, 144–145 Stefan Bollmann, 148L S. Bollmann, 151T S. Bollmann, 153 Markus Felix 1 PushingPixels, 156–157 Atamari, 156B S. Bollmann, 157B Cecil, 163T Staff Sgt. Daniel Yarnall, 170TR Vassil, 172T Michaelandrewl, 174L S. Bollmann, 176 In twilight, 177T Nonexyst, 177L, Alterna2, 179 S. Bollmann, 181R S. Bollmann, 183L Sven Mandel, 183R Penner, 184–185 IllaZilla, 188T Sven Mandel, 188B S. Bollmann, 189 Llann Wé2, 191 S. Bollmann, 193 musicisentropy, 196 Denis Apel, 197L cat_collector, 202 Dominik Matus, 207B Shadowgate, 207T Andreas Lawen, Fotandi, 209 John Walsh, 209TR Jim Summaria, 214T Swimfinfan, 214B Frank Schwichtenberg, 215 I, Jaakonam, 216T Bruno Bergamini, 217T Andreas Lawen, 220 Dark Apostrophe, 221T Florian Stangl

BAND INDEX